Lancashire
Edited by Annabel Cook

First published in Great Britain in 2008 by:
Young Writers
Remus House
Coltsfoot Drive
Peterborough
PE2 9JX
Telephone: 01733 890066
Website: www.youngwriters.co.uk

All Rights Reserved

© *Copyright Contributors 2008*

SB ISBN 978-1 84431 618 2

Foreword

Young Writers was established in 1991 and has been passionately devoted to the promotion of reading and writing in children and young adults ever since. The quest continues today. Young Writers remains as committed to the nurturing of poetic and literary talent as ever.

This year's Young Writers competition has proven as vibrant and dynamic as ever and we are delighted to present a showcase of the best poetry from across the UK and in some cases overseas. Each poem has been selected from a wealth of *Little Laureates 2008* entries before ultimately being published in this, our seventeenth primary school poetry series.

Once again, we have been supremely impressed by the overall quality of the entries we have received. The imagination, energy and creativity which has gone into each young writer's entry made choosing the poems a challenging and often difficult but ultimately hugely rewarding task - the general high standard of the work submitted ensured this opportunity to bring their poetry to a larger appreciative audience.

We sincerely hope you are pleased with this final collection and that you will enjoy *Little Laureates 2008 Lancashire* for many years to come.

Contents

Sophia Rawlings (6)   1

Asmall Primary School, Ormskirk
Adam Harper (9)	1
Jacob Ball (9)	2
Rebecca Hughes (10)	2
Owen Edwards (10)	3
Robert Thomas (10)	3
Melissa Buckley (11)	4
Rebecca Lewis (9)	4

Clarendon Primary School, Bolton
Asha Patel (10)	4
Safwan Patel (10)	5
Brandon Collins (10)	5
Shabana Haji (10)	6
Muhammad Mogra (10)	6
Asma Dalal (10)	7
Ayesha Patel (10)	7
Noor-Muhammed Sadik (11)	8
Hannaan Pathan (11)	8
Than Dar (10)	9
Adnan Kaduji (10)	9
Sheema Patel (10)	10
Fatimah Patel (10)	10

Garstang Community Primary School, Preston
Ellie Jolleys (10)	11

Hawthorns Junior School, Blackburn
Hafsa Nisar (8)	11
Juwairiyyah Mubarak (8)	12
Aymun Rashid (9)	12
Adnan Hussain (10)	12
Omar Malik (9)	13
Zaynah Salam (8)	13
Arshad Ahmed (9)	13

Zainab Shah (9)	14
Amina Hussain (8)	14
Memnat Shah (8)	14
Aisha Patel (9)	15
Khadijah Patel (9)	15
Muhammad Sitponya (8)	16
Maryam Survery (8)	16
Sharafat Moosa (8)	16
Saima Naz (9)	17
Saifali Patel (9)	17

Hodge Clough Junior School, Oldham

Jasmine McKnight (9)	17
Jordan Bohanna (9)	18
Joe Mooney (8)	18
Lauren Taylor (9)	19
Amy Taylor (8)	19
Chloe Boswell (9)	20
Ellie Taylor (9)	20
Molly Taylor (8)	21
Olivia Graham (8)	21
Jessica Lane (8)	22
Emily Stone (8)	22
Daniel Woodcock (8)	23
Adam Turner (8)	23
Dylan Collinson (11)	24
Chloe Campbell (11)	24
Jessi Wolfenden (10)	25
Kirsty Hazeltine (11)	25
Sarah Jane Callender (10)	26
Helena Clarke (10)	26
Shannon Withey (11)	27
Andrew Jones (10)	27
Adena Dewar (11)	28
Laura McAll (10)	28
Courtney Graves (11)	29
Rachael Smith (11)	29
Jamie Pollinger (11)	30
Alix Withey (11)	30
Ryan Bishop (8)	31
Megan James (9)	31

Jack Unsworth (8)	32
Eleanor Symons (8)	32
Chloe Cook (9)	33
Emily Mott (9)	33
Jessica Walker (8)	34
Jane Brayshaw (8)	34
Jessica Paul (9)	35
Olivia Bland (9)	35
Chloe Fleming (8), Wesley Woodhead,	
Jordan Lowe & Darrell Kershaw (7)	36
Adrian Salt (8)	36
Kara McKune (7)	37
Harriet Wharfe (7)	37
Jayden Moxam (8)	38
Molly Roebuck (8)	38
Poppy Greenough (7)	39
Ben Holroyd (8)	39
Morgan Crossley (8) & Rachael Pollinger (7)	40
Cameron Holland (7) & Elysse Graves (8)	40
Victoria Costello (7)	41
George Crawford (7)	41
Cameron Whitworth (7)	42
Joshua Whitehill (7)	42
Ethan Weeks (7)	43
Amy Shanley (7)	43
Caitlin Feeney (7)	44
Sam Sykes (9)	44
Samuel Biggs (9)	45
John Lord (9)	45
Alysha Brown (9)	46
Morgan Rustidge (10)	46
Hannah Hopkins (10)	47
Kate Matthews (10)	47
Liam Tasker (9)	48
Charmaine Barney (10)	48
Bryan Pitcher (9)	49
Zac Stansfield (10)	49
Megan Ashton (10)	50
Tia Bell (10)	50
Jordan Heywood (10)	51
Joseph Wharfe (10)	51

Sascha Langley (9) 52
Thomas Wareing (9) 52

Lammack Primary School, Blackburn
Humairaa Ismail (8) 53
Khadeejah Abdulla (8) 53
Zain Mathiya (8) 54
Aamirah Patel (8) 55
Muhammad Motala (8) 55
Amirah Desai (8) 56
Tayaab Al-Hassan (8) 56
Farah Musa (8) 56
Fatimah Dasu (8) 57
Heraa Arif (8) 57
Ismail Namaji (8) 57
Usaamah Ougradar (8) 58
Zaahirah Patel (8) 58

Markland Hill Primary School, Bolton
Asena Akdeniz (8) 59
Isobel Tailor (8) 59
Emma Jo Parr (9) 60
Yunqi Li (8) 60
William Gorman (9) 60
Molly Magee (9) 61
James Whalley (9) 61
Thomas Cummins (9) 61
Alice Entwistle (9) 62
Millie Dawson (9) 62
Calum Smith (9) 62
Luke Charnock (9) 63
Myles Crofts (9) 63
Matthew Bates (9) 63
Sarah Minney (9) 64
Elizabeth Wood (9) 64
Mohammed Nadat (8) 64
Jack Bannister (8) 65
Sam Hassall (8) 65
Ghalib Hashmi (9) 65
Julia Sabery (11) 66
Alexandra Darbyshire (10) 66

Scott Corrigan (10)	66
Rebecca Vincent (8)	67
Gracelyn Byrne (9)	67
Eleanor Goulding (9)	67
Heather Walton (9)	68
Jessica Dhodakia (9)	68
Elizabeth Waudby (9)	69
Aimee Parr (7)	69
Edward Fisher (8)	70
Hassan Baz (11)	70
Khadija Amla (10)	70
Leila Safi (11)	71
Muhammad Karim (11)	71
Nathan Dhodakia (11)	71
Ellie McGivern (10)	72
Eleanor Schenk (11)	72
Jennifer Walmsley (11)	72
Charlotte Bannister (11)	73
Ross Tracey (9)	73
Bradley Light (11)	73
Priya Guhathakurta (7)	74
Thomas Mair (8)	74
Megan Halsall (10)	75
Lucy Entwistle (10)	75

Nateby Primary School, Preston

Dan Green (7)	75
Abbie Hewitt (7)	76
Faye Taylor-McCormick (8)	76
Josh Mitchell (7)	76
Sam Collinson (8)	77
Freddie Hewitt (9)	77
Chloe May Illingworth (7)	77
Olivia Barlow (8)	78
Finlay Bracken (7)	78
Alice Danson (8)	79
Robert Slater (7)	79
Harriet Kelsall (8)	80
Rachel Bell (9)	80
Peter Walton (9)	81
Eleanor Moss (8)	81

Hannah Lawrenson (8) 82
James Davis (8) 82

Overton St Helen's CE School, Overton
Jade Mashiter (8) 82
Tom Morbey (8) 83
Natalie Mason-Brown (9) 83
Aimee Bailey (8) 83
Eve Abdel Moneim (8) 84
George Higginson (8) 84
Grace Abdel Moneim (8) 85
Roger Mall (8) 85
Wilk Morbey (8) 86
Oliver Whitehead (9) 86
Lily Fegan (8) 87
Anna Hebblewhite (8) 87
Hannah Jackson (9) 88
Kathryn Barrett (8) 88
Rebecca Wakefield (9) 89
Jaimie O'Brien (9) 89
George Higginson (8) 90
Marnie Cvetkovic-Jones (8) 90
Amelia Glackin-Melici (7) 91
Kelsey Hadwin (9) 91
Jaimie O'Brien (9) 91

St Agnes CE Primary School, Longsight
Samra Shahbaz (11) 92
Fahad Hussain (10) 92
Sadia Khan (9) 93
Delwar Kabir (10) 94
Ahsan Anwar (10) 94
Bilal Imran (10) 95
Maaria Ahmad (10) 95
Sabah Afzal (11) 96
Sadikur Rahman (10) 97
Maria Stokes (10) 98
Yasmina Akhter (10) 98
Aliyah Begum (9) 99

Habib Tajwar (10)	99
Amina Rahman (10)	100

St James' CE Primary School, Clitheroe

Morgan Robinson (8)	100
Lillian Nuttall (8)	101
Chloe Ross (8)	101
Xanthe Taylor (9)	102
Rachel Harnick (9)	102
Cameron Starkie (8)	103
James Scorah (7)	103
Chloe Warburton (7)	104
Olivia Houghton (8)	104
Jenna-Alexandra Sefton-Bell (8)	105

St Joseph's Catholic Primary School, Wigan

Abigail Prescott (10)	105
Libby Bennett (9)	105
Meghan Pollitt (10)	106

St Mary's CE (A) School, Saddleworth

Ruby Duncan (10)	107
Fionn Wall (10)	107
Kate Gardner (10)	108

Whittle-Le-Woods CE Primary School, Chorley

Rebecca Baxendale (7)	108
Emma Dixon (7)	109
Morgan Cooper (7)	109
Jordan Rushton (8)	110
Anna Billingsley (7)	110
Oliver Darby (8)	110
Olivia Wilkes (8)	111
Sam Barber (7)	111
Deagan Greenacre (7)	111
Rebecca Bamber (8)	112
Ben Hall (8)	112
John Bennett (7)	112
Harvey Fisher (8)	113
Jessica Buff (7)	113

Alex Fairhurst (7)   113
Sadie Gowan (7)   114
Katie Barlow (7)   114

Withnell Fold Primary School, Chorley
Sophie Ruth Fowler (10)   114
Gabriela Sharp (10)   115
Lewis Hawkes (10)   115
Zoë Mather (9)   116
Lucy Davis (11)   116
Isobel Ryde (10)   117
James Guy (10)   117
Joanna Nicholas (10)   118
Davie Beesley (10)   118
Emily Chaplin (10)   119
Amy Wood (9)   119
Lois Waterhouse (9)   120
Charlie Adams (10)   120
Fergus Tallon (11)   121
Josh Eckersley (11)   121
Kai Fox (10)   122

The Poems

Sophia's Special Poem

I just love being in the arms
Of my mummy and daddy
Because I love them that much
All my hugs and kisses I get
I keep them in my heart forever
And never forget them when time goes past
And I love them!

Sophia Rawlings (6)

If

If I won the lottery
I would buy a £300,000 mansion
And get 300 bulldogs as guards.

If I won the lottery
I would buy a Ferrari Spider with leather seats
And steering wheel made of leather.

If I won the lottery
I would buy a steam train and railway in America.

If I won the lottery
I would buy Disneyland, Florida.

If I won the lottery
I would buy a black Bentley.

If I won the lottery
I would buy a big, massive limousine.

Adam Harper (9)
Asmall Primary School, Ormskirk

If

If I won the lottery
I would buy England Football Club and become manager.

If I won the lottery
I would buy a Bentley car and a Lamborghini.

If I won the lottery
I would give a home to people without one.

If I won the lottery
I would buy a new house.

If I won the lottery
I would put a fairground in the garden.

If I won the lottery
I would buy two dogs.

But most of all
I would shut down all the schools.

Jacob Ball (9)
Asmall Primary School, Ormskirk

Summer

The sun is like a burning giant on a hot summer's day
Ice creams melting like you only have the cone
Pools like big, cool ponds that you can fall into
Surf like wild horses galloping in the sea
Jugs of melting ice like icebergs melting into the sea
Dolphins acting elegantly like swans
BBQs are like hot metals burning all your food.

Rebecca Hughes (10)
Asmall Primary School, Ormskirk

Pain

I am pain,
Spreading across the Earth as a shadow,
Stabbing people so they scream.
I am pain,
Part of Hell.
I am always inside you,
Waiting to be released,
I help death to come,
You cannot get rid of me.
I love to watch you cry and crumple to the floor.
I am pain,
Part of Hell.

Owen Edwards (10)
Asmall Primary School, Ormskirk

Misery

I am misery,
Spreading death upon the Earth.
I am misery,
Releasing my nasty curse.
I am misery,
Handing out stings, bites and pain
And when you think you're free,
I'll come to you again.
I am misery,
The everlasting enemy.
I am misery.

Robert Thomas (10)
Asmall Primary School, Ormskirk

Joy

Joy is like a lamb leaping in spring.
Joy is like children playing in the snow.
Joy is like the end of the school year.
Joy is like a beautiful flower.
Joy is like your dream house.
Joy is like your first birthday.
Joy is like a newborn baby's smile.
Joy is always there.

Melissa Buckley (11)
Asmall Primary School, Ormskirk

Death

Death sounds like a storm in your body
Death smells like rotting eggs
Death feels like a knife pulling your heart out
Death tastes like charcoal
Death looks like a rainy day
Death lives in the Devil's cave.

Rebecca Lewis (9)
Asmall Primary School, Ormskirk

My Favourite Things

Chatting to my mates
And baking cakes,
Playing outside
And having lots of fun.

Buying lots of sweets
And playing some beats,
Having loads of fun
And bathing in the sun.

Asha Patel (10)
Clarendon Primary School, Bolton

My Favourite Thing

S wimming is marvellous and healthy
W et but passionate
I n the pool it's cold, but hot
M oving about in the water, how happy I feel
M uch I need to tell you about swimming,
    I can't tell you about everything
I 've done a mile, but am trying to swim the English Channel
N obody can outswim me!
G oing to the baths, how excited I am,
    but when I come out, how cold I am!

Safwan Patel (10)
Clarendon Primary School, Bolton

My Favourite Things

Rugby is the best
Better than the rest
Football is as well
Maybe golf might ring a bell.

Bowling is just as fun
Maybe you would like a chocolate bun
Ice skating is cool
If you fall down you feel like a fool.

Tennis is mint
If you want I'll give you a hint
Watching TV is not that bad
Watching wrestling makes me glad.

Brandon Collins (10)
Clarendon Primary School, Bolton

My Favourite Things

Playing outside is great
Because you can play with your mate,
But my mum has to bake
For a super birthday cake.

In the evening I have to eat,
Just a creamy biscuit and some tea
And I watch TV,
My favourite programme is Disney.

Outside is dark
And then I hear a dog bark.
I have my cosy socks
To go to sleep in the dark.

When I wake up,
I have a funny look.
Then I get dressed up
And then I come downstairs to cook.

Shabana Haji (10)
Clarendon Primary School, Bolton

My Favourite Things

F ootball is great
A n aeroplane is fun to ride on
V ikings are fun to learn about
O pening a present is fantastic
U nder my table is an unbelievable hiding place
R iding on my bike
I ce skating is fun
T asting different foods
E very night I play on the laptop.

Muhammad Mogra (10)
Clarendon Primary School, Bolton

My Favourite Things

Playing outside is great
Because you can play with your mates,
But my mum has to bake
For her birthday cake.

Playing games is fun,
But in the game you need to run,
But someone comes along and it's my mum.

When I go to school,
It's very cool,
Later I have to go home,
But then I moan.

Outside is dark,
Then I hear a dog bark,
Then I go and walk
Near to a rock.

Asma Dalal (10)
Clarendon Primary School, Bolton

My Favourite Things

Friends are fun to play with
They are really, really great
Even though we break up sometimes
We always get through it.

My friends are always beside me
Take care when I am sad
And whenever we break up
We feel really bad.

My friends are just the best
They are better than all the rest.

Ayesha Patel (10)
Clarendon Primary School, Bolton

My Favourite Person

Sister, my sister,
How glad am I,
To have you here,
Just by my bed, so near.

I may be awful,
I may be bad,
But still you are
In my loving heart.

I have the love
For you from above,
For only I know
How much I love.

Sister, my beloved
Let us now be friends,
For only I know
How much I love.

Noor-Muhammed Sadik (11)
Clarendon Primary School, Bolton

Hobbies

H elping is one of my helpful hobbies
O veracting is one too
B oats are what I like, especially the Navy's
B irds are what I love, especially when they go *cuckoo*
I ce skating is cool, but when I fall I am a fool
E lephants are fascinating, I also like the zoo
S o what is your hobby? Yes, I'm asking you!

Hannaan Pathan (11)
Clarendon Primary School, Bolton

My Favourite Things

Swimming comes first,
Swimming is the best,
It's the best sport, out of the rest.

Reading comes second,
Reading is fun,
Without reading, you could be dumb.

Dancing comes third,
Dancing gives you a beat,
Although when you dance, your body starts to heat.

Parties come fourth,
Parties are great,
You're missing the fun if you come late.

I'm a friend,
A daughter,
A sister and a niece.

My colour is blue,
Because of who I am,
Daring, happy, sad, excited, nervous and mixed feelings.

As you can see, I'm being me,
Because this is my . . .
Identity.

Than Dar (10)
Clarendon Primary School, Bolton

My Favourite Thing

C atches win matches
R uns earn points
I n the field running wild
C ricketers are mild
K illing each other to get the hit
E ating right to keep fit
T oday will be the day to see it.

Adnan Kaduji (10)
Clarendon Primary School, Bolton

My Favourite Things

My favourite things are very big in quantity
Memories, emotions and family
Teachers, friends, so many people around me
So many people care for me
These are my favourite things

My favourite things are so much fun
It is so hard keeping away from them

My favourite things are very big in quantity
There are so many calm things around me
Going on the computer, reading in the sun
All these things are so much fun
These are my favourite things

My favourite things are so much fun
It is so hard keeping away from them
My favourite things are so much fun
It is so hard keeping away from them.

Sheema Patel (10)
Clarendon Primary School, Bolton

My Favourite Things

Friends are fun whatever you do,
Playing games and laughing with you,
Helping you in whatever you do,
Always there to chat with you,
Playing on our bikes
And going on a hike,
That's why they're called 'good' friends.

Fatimah Patel (10)
Clarendon Primary School, Bolton

Me And You, You And Me!

You smell of a freshly cut meadow
Your eyes are the deepest pools
Never-ending
Telling tales of mysteries long ago.
When you move you are a silk scarf
Swaying, shimmering in the warm breeze
Shiny, soft, smooth, sleek.
Our games are full of mischief and mayhem
Equals, quits, a team.
When you are scared, I am brave
When you are sad my sadness hurts
Like a knife going through my heart
When in perfect harmony
They say we are 'poetry in motion'.
We are as one
My pony and me!

Ellie Jolleys (10)
Garstang Community Primary School, Preston

Love

Love is like a bundle of hearts
Love is not a flock of darts
It makes you smell like a little red rose
But sometimes it makes you have a red nose
Love sounds like a twirling bird singing
But sometimes it sounds like a doorbell ringing
Love is pink like dreaming stars
It tastes like tasty bars
Love feels like snowflakes in the air
But it doesn't feel like a big bear!

Hafsa Nisar (8)
Hawthorns Junior School, Blackburn

Darkness

Darkness is grey as the stormy clouds,
It tastes like an old cigarette,
It smells of smoke,
It looks as if someone's died,
It sounds like someone is screaming and screeching,
It feels like blood,
It reminds me of a vampire.

Juwairiyyah Mubarak (8)
Hawthorns Junior School, Blackburn

Love

Love is red like paint
It tastes like a fresh bowl of fruit
It smells like a fresh flower that has just been grown
Love looks like a love heart
Love sounds like some jazzy music
It feels like happiness
It reminds me of my mum.

Aymun Rashid (9)
Hawthorns Junior School, Blackburn

Wish

Close in your hand
A spark from the sun
A moon's lost silver
A crow's black feather
The heart of a star
And *wish!*

Adnan Hussain (10)
Hawthorns Junior School, Blackburn

Fear

Fear is like a black, stormy hole
It tastes like damp fruit
It smells like musty, damp toast
It looks like a dark, lonely road
It sounds like crawling footsteps
It feels like being alone
It reminds me of *fear!*

Omar Malik (9)
Hawthorns Junior School, Blackburn

Love

Love is as red as an apple,
It tastes like a tap of water,
It smells as fresh as lavender,
It looks like a flock of birds flying gracefully,
It sounds like some peaceful music,
It feels like a relaxed house,
It reminds me of my mum and dad.

Zaynah Salam (8)
Hawthorns Junior School, Blackburn

Fear

Fear is as black as space
It tastes like cold rice
It smells rusty and smoky
It looks like a dark forest
It sounds like a ghost howling
It reminds me of a bloodsucking vampire.

Arshad Ahmed (9)
Hawthorns Junior School, Blackburn

Love

Love is as red as a rose.
It tastes like bunches of sweets.
It smells like lots of fresh flowers.
It looks like a big flock of birds hugging.
It sounds like two bees buzzing.
It feels like lips on your cheeks.
It reminds me of my parents kissing and hugging me.

Zainab Shah (9)
Hawthorns Junior School, Blackburn

Fun

Fun is yellow as a sunflower
Fun tastes like a sprinkle of sugar
Fun smells like a spray of air freshener
It looks like a cute baby
Fun sounds like a little three-year-old laughing
Fun feels like babies' skin
Fun reminds you of your lovely, caring friends!

Amina Hussain (8)
Hawthorns Junior School, Blackburn

Happiness

Happiness is as pink as a flower
It tastes like fresh berries
It smells like red roses
It looks like a beautiful garden
It sounds like birds singing in the trees
It feels like we're in a funfair
It reminds me of my wonderful friends.

Memnat Shah (8)
Hawthorns Junior School, Blackburn

The Poem Of Seasons

Spring is the time of year,
When flowers pop out from their buds.

Summer is the time of year,
When everybody goes out on vacations.

Autumn is the time of year,
When leaves fall down from the trees.

But winter is the coldest time of year,
Because there are always snowflakes falling from the cloudy sky.

All the seasons are fun,
Because there is always something there waiting for you.

Aisha Patel (9)
Hawthorns Junior School, Blackburn

The Seasonal Poem

Spring is the time of year when the flowers pop out
And feel the breeze.

Summer is the time of year when people go out
And enjoy the sun.

Autumn is a time of the year where the colourful leaves
Fall gently from the trees.

But winter is the time when snow comes
And people go out to play with the snow.

All of the seasons are good
Because there is always something fun to do!

Khadijah Patel (9)
Hawthorns Junior School, Blackburn

Winter

Winter is a cold crystal
Jack Frost has been
Nothing to be seen
It's a blank sheet of paper
A season gripped
Winter is a cold crystal.

Muhammad Sitponya (8)
Hawthorns Junior School, Blackburn

Love

Love is as red as a heart
It tastes like sugar spreading in your mouth
It smells like a creamy cake
It looks like Valentine's Day
It sounds like people are singing
It feels like chocolate melting in your hands
It reminds me of when I was born!

Maryam Survery (8)
Hawthorns Junior School, Blackburn

Fear

Fear is grey as a foggy day
It tastes like a tornado
It smells distasteful and damp
It looks like a lonely castle
It sounds like a thunder night
It feels like a flock of clouds
It reminds me of a stormy day.

Sharafat Moosa (8)
Hawthorns Junior School, Blackburn

Happiness

Happiness is red as a rose
It tastes like a bowl of fresh fruit
It smells like a chocolate cake
It looks like Christmas
It sounds like birds singing
It feels like water in a hand
It reminds me of my kind friends.

Saima Naz (9)
Hawthorns Junior School, Blackburn

Fear

Fear is darker than the Earth
It tastes like blood
It smells like stinkbugs
It looks like bats
It sounds like wind howling
It feels like vampires sucking blood
It reminds me of horror movies.

Saifali Patel (9)
Hawthorns Junior School, Blackburn

Eco Schools

If you dump things in the water,
You are polluting the fish.
Help clean the world by recycling.
Save energy by turning off computers and lights.
Plant trees to produce oxygen.
Look after our school grounds.

Jasmine McKnight (9)
Hodge Clough Junior School, Oldham

Eco Warrior

Light helper
Energy saver
Pollution stopper
Litter reducer
Oxygen maker
Life saver
Tap stopper
Tree saver
Tree helper
Environment helper
Heat saver
Tree protector
Pollution reducer
Best recycler
Fuel preventer
Ozone layer
Litter detector
Tree planter
Light switcher
Carbon dioxide decreaser
Oxygen preventer
It's our matter.

Jordan Bohanna (9)
Hodge Clough Junior School, Oldham

Eco School

Litter collector
Light switcher offer
Everyone's helper
Tree saver
Ozone layer
Animal liker
That's an eco warrior.

Joe Mooney (8)
Hodge Clough Junior School, Oldham

Eco Schools

E nergy saving
C ollecting rubbish
O wn the rubbish

S top smoking
C omputers off
H elp the environment
O wn environment
O xygen helps us breathe
L ocal area
S witch off lights.

Lauren Taylor (9)
Hodge Clough Junior School, Oldham

Eco Schools

E nergy saver
C are for the environment
O xygen comes from trees

S aving everything
C ans recycled
H elp the environment
O ff go the lights
O il, don't let it get into seas
L eaves give us oxygen
S tart switching off computers.

Amy Taylor (8)
Hodge Clough Junior School, Oldham

Eco Schools

E njoy our environment
C hildren need a better home
O xygen

S top smoking
C are for the environment
H elp the environment
O ff with lights
O il spills are dangerous
L ights off
S tart saving schools.

Chloe Boswell (9)
Hodge Clough Junior School, Oldham

Eco Schools

E xpand your recycling
C omputers, turn them off
O xygen, we need it

S eas, don't pollute them
C are for the environment
H omes need to save electricity
O ff with lights
O ur local area needs saving
L itter, put it in the bin
S tart saving energy.

Ellie Taylor (9)
Hodge Clough Junior School, Oldham

Eco Schools

E very child help the environment
C ountryside helper
O xygen trees

S tart saving electricity
C are for the environment
H elp saving the world
O ff with the lights
O wn environment
L ight saver
S oon stop.

Molly Taylor (8)
Hodge Clough Junior School, Oldham

Eco School

E nergy saver
C omputers need turning off
O vercoming stubborn attitudes

S tart being an eco warrior
C onserve energy
H ave less electricity
O il makes lots of pollution, so stop
O xygen, we need it
L ights off.

Olivia Graham (8)
Hodge Clough Junior School, Oldham

Eco Schools

E lectricity should not be wasted
C old countries getting hotter
O il being spilt

S ave our planet
C hildren need a nice place to live
H eating being wasted
O ff with the lights
O xygen comes from trees
L eaves help us breathe
S ave our environment.

Jessica Lane (8)
Hodge Clough Junior School, Oldham

Eco Schools

E lectricty off overnight
C hildren deserve a nice place to live
O xygen, we need it

S tart recycling
C are for the environment
H elp save the world
O ff lights to save energy
O il kills trees
L ittering is not helping the environment
S top littering!

Emily Stone (8)
Hodge Clough Junior School, Oldham

Eco Schools

E is for energy saver
C is for can recycler
O is for our own environment

S is for start to switch off lights
C is for conserve energy
H is for having a clean world
O is for our health
O is for oil off transport
L is for littering is not appropriate
S is for seas which are full of oil.

Daniel Woodcock (8)
Hodge Clough Junior School, Oldham

Eco Schools

E nergy saver
C omputer power
O ff switch

S top carbon monoxide
C old countries getting warmer
H ome saving
O il stop
O xygen saver
L ight saving
S top pollution.

Adam Turner (8)
Hodge Clough Junior School, Oldham

Eco Schools

E very day we recycle thousands
C ardboard, paper, glass and cars
O ld tyres can be recycled too

S chools recycle to help you
C ars can also be recycled
H appy faces all around
O pen up the recycling bin
O ur world can be tidy
L andfills are overflowing
S ave the animals and the environment.

Dylan Collinson (11)
Hodge Clough Junior School, Oldham

Eco Schools

E very day you should recycle
C an you recycle?
O ur environment is dying

S ave our planet
C ompost can be used again
H elp our planet
O ld tyres need recycling
O ur homes are carbon footprinted
L ose the bins and start recycling
S ave your home.

Chloe Campbell (11)
Hodge Clough Junior School, Oldham

Eco Schools

E lectricity cannot be recycled
C o-operate in recycling
O ur planet needs to be loved

S end the message around the world
C arbon footprint is how much energy you waste
H elp our world live
O ur planet needs your help
O ver 28 million people still throw away rubbish instead of recycling
L itter will eventually cover the planet
S ave the planet!

Jessi Wolfenden (10)
Hodge Clough Junior School, Oldham

Eco Schools

E co-friendly people
C are for the environment
O nly using electricity when you need it

S ave the world from more pollution
C an you recycle?
H elp us look after the world
O r just become green
O ld tyres can be recycled
L andfills are getting bigger, taking up more grass
S o help us please to make our world last!

Kirsty Hazeltine (11)
Hodge Clough Junior School, Oldham

Eco Schools

E nergy saving should be a craving,
   so start it fast so our energy can last.
C ompost bins we need, to get rid of those weeds.
O ur world needs green, instead of us being mean.

S chool grounds we need to care for,
   because we all know littering is against the law.
C are for this place, it's better than leaving it as a disgrace.
H elp us look after this world.
O nly walk far, so you don't use a car.
O pen up the bus station and save our nation!
L et's recycle more, then it will be green galore.
S ave this world and help others as well as yourself.

Sarah Jane Callender (10)
Hodge Clough Junior School, Oldham

Eco Schools

E very day you should recycle
C an save energy for our homes
O ld tyres worn out

S ave our planet
C ars that are really rusty
H elp us reuse it again and again
O ur energy makes global warming
O ur school recycles
L ots of things can be recycled
S o it's up to you now!

Helena Clarke (10)
Hodge Clough Junior School, Oldham

Eco Schools

E nvironment matters
C ardboard you can recycle
O ld tyres too

S o open up your green bin
C ars that are rusty
H elp recycle
O pen up your recycle bin
O ld Christmas cards too
L andfills are growing bigger and bigger
S o save the Earth.

Shannon Withey (11)
Hodge Clough Junior School, Oldham

Eco Schools

E verybody matters
C an you make a difference?
O ur recycled paper is a life saver

S chools will save our minds
C arbon footprints are to be reduced
H azardous chemicals in the air
O ldham schools are the best
O ur children can be saved
L andfills drool, recycling rules
S uper recycler.

Andrew Jones (10)
Hodge Clough Junior School, Oldham

Eco Schools

E arth matters!
C arbon footprints are too big
O ur waste is damaging the earth

S ome people don't recycle, why?
C ould we do more for the Earth?
H ow could we change? Recycle!
O ur planet is dying
O nly we can save it
L ove your planet, don't kill it!
S ave energy, save the Earth!

Adena Dewar (11)
Hodge Clough Junior School, Oldham

Eco Schools

E co friendly
C an save energy
O ld tyres can be recycled

S ave our planet, global warming
C ars that are rusty should be recycled
H ouse warmth, insulate
O ur school recycles
O ur streets will be clean if you recycle
L itter on the streets should be cleaned
S chools mainly recycle paper.

Laura McAll (10)
Hodge Clough Junior School, Oldham

Eco Schools

E lectricity can always be saved
C an you recycle? It's easy!
O ur planet needs us

S o start recycling now
C ome on and recycle
H ave you helped at all?
O xygen is in trees, stop cutting them
O ur planet will be great
L ove green
S ave the planet!

Courtney Graves (11)
Hodge Clough Junior School, Oldham

Eco Schools

E arth matters
C arbon footprint is family waste
O ur planet is dying

S ave energy
C overing the planet in rubbish, not cool!
H ow did the world get so messy?
O ur planet is becoming a dump
O ld things can be made into new again
L ove the Earth
S ave the Earth!

Rachael Smith (11)
Hodge Clough Junior School, Oldham

Eco Schools

E verybody matters when it comes to recycling
C limate change is on the way
O zone layer is being destroyed every day

S top polluting the environment
C arbon footprints need to be reduced now!
H azardous chemicals are released into the atmosphere every day
O nly use recyclable materials
O ur planet can still be saved
L andfill drools, recycling rules!
S tand up for what is right.

Jamie Pollinger (11)
Hodge Clough Junior School, Oldham

Eco Schools

E nvironment matters
C ompost/manure helps
O nly use your car when you need it

S o reuse
C ompost bins help
H elp the world to be a better place
O pen your green bin
O ld tyres can be recycled
L ess electricity, more money
S ave the water.

Alix Withey (11)
Hodge Clough Junior School, Oldham

Eco School

Help us now
By saving electricity.
Turn off lights and computers.
Save paper so there are more trees to provide oxygen for us.
Don't leave taps on, it will waste water.
Help people to stop dumping rubbish in lakes and rivers.
Ride a bike to school or walk to help the ozone layer,
It will also keep you fit.
Throw your litter in the bin.
If you do something for the world,
The world will do something for you!

Ryan Bishop (8)
Hodge Clough Junior School, Oldham

Eco School

E co school
C all us in
O ut of the gloom we come

S topping global warming
C ollecting rubbish
H indering pollution
O zone layer
O nly use things when it's serious
L ights switching (click).

Megan James (9)
Hodge Clough Junior School, Oldham

Eco School

E mergency for protecting our environment
C ollecting litter and rubbish
O K environment

S earching for litter that's on the floor
C aring for our planet
H aving a good and tidy playground
O nly caring about protecting the environment
O ld rubbish, got to pick up
L earning to protect the environment.

Jack Unsworth (8)
Hodge Clough Junior School, Oldham

Eco Schools

E lectricity needs saving
C aring is needed on Earth
O nly cut down the amount of trees needed

S ave water by turning off the tap after use
C an you please stop throwing litter on the floor?
H elp us recycle clothes, paper and cans
O ld things don't just go in the bin, reuse them
O nly turn the computer on when needed
L ights must be turned off if not in use
S o be an eco school.

Eleanor Symons (8)
Hodge Clough Junior School, Oldham

Eco School

Don't waste water
Stop the dripping taps

Pick up litter,
Find a bin and put it in,
But make sure you recycle your paper,
Plastics and cans.

Jog, run, ride or walk,
But don't use cars
Because it is destroying the ozone layer.

Save us from the bad gases
That are polluting the world.

So that's how to be an eco school.

Chloe Cook (9)
Hodge Clough Junior School, Oldham

Eco School

Eco warrior
Power saver
Litter collector
Light switcher
Oxygen maker
Tree planter
Carbon decreaser
Ozone layer
Ozone warrior
Save our world.

Emily Mott (9)
Hodge Clough Junior School, Oldham

Eco School

Stop letting the water drip from your taps
Ban people from leaving taps running.

Recycle waste, recycle waste
Recycle your paper, cans and plastics.

School grounds, school grounds
Pick up the rubbish and put it in the bins.

Look after the world, look after the world
And the world will look after us.

Jessica Walker (8)
Hodge Clough Junior School, Oldham

Eco Schools

Tree planter
Not a waster
Can recycler
Light switcher
Environment helper
Oxygen breather
Life saver
Earth protector
Now or never
Eco school forever.

Jane Brayshaw (8)
Hodge Clough Junior School, Oldham

Eco School

Stop using electricity by turning off computers, lights and TV.
Turn off running taps and look after rivers, streams and seas.
Pick up litter around the world and recycle your paper, glass
                                                              and plastics.
Walk to school, it will keep you fit.
Don't use buses, cars and trains, more ozone layer.
You should water plants and trees because they will provide us
                                                    with oxygen to breathe
Follow these rules and you can be an eco school.

Jessica Paul (9)
Hodge Clough Junior School, Oldham

Eco Schools

Light saver
Environment helper
Paper sorter
World liker
Rubbish collector
Ozone layer
Light switcher
Tree planter
Oxygen breather
Protect our world
Fuel preventer.

Olivia Bland (9)
Hodge Clough Junior School, Oldham

Eco Schools

E nvironment saving
C ollecting rubbish that people drop
O nly use things when you need to

S ave water, turn off the tap
C oming to school on your feet
H owever, we can save electricity
O nly putting litter in the recycling bin
O r use it again and again
L itter picking
S topping people from wasting energy.

Chloe Fleming (8), Wesley Woodhead, Jordan Lowe & Darrell Kershaw (7)
Hodge Clough Junior School, Oldham

Eco Schools

E co warriors
C lean water
O nly using what's needed

S aving our environment
C aring for our world
H elping electricity
O ver again turn off the light
O ver again recycle
L itter is bad to throw
S top littering.

Adrian Salt (8)
Hodge Clough Junior School, Oldham

Eco Schools

E lectricity saving
C lean up
O r ask the owner to clean it up

S top people from throwing litter on the floor
C aring for one another
H opefully they'll clean it up themselves
O ld tyres and rusty cars, we could recycle
O pen your eyes
L ook after the environment
S ave water.

Kara McKune (7)
Hodge Clough Junior School, Oldham

Eco Schools

E nergy savings
C ollecting waste
O nly using what's needed

S top throwing rubbish on the floor
C are for the school
H elping the planet
O ld things, use them again
O ver again, turn off the tap
L ook after the environment
S ave trees.

Harriet Wharfe (7)
Hodge Clough Junior School, Oldham

Eco Schools

E is for eco warriors
C is for driving cars is dangerous for the air
O pening your eyes

S top throwing litter
C an you stop leaving the tap on!
H aving no litter
O nly put the light on when you need it
O ld things go in the bin
L is for loading things into the bin
S ave trees.

Jayden Moxam (8)
Hodge Clough Junior School, Oldham

Eco Schools

E nergy saving
C aring for the school
O nly use water when needed

S top throwing litter
C are for the environment
H elping the land
O ld things take to the recycling bank
O r keep them
L itter is bad
S ave trees.

Molly Roebuck (8)
Hodge Clough Junior School, Oldham

Eco Schools

E lectricity saving
C ollecting rubbish
O nly using what's needed

S aving our world
C leaning rubbish
H orrible mess
O nly save the world
O nly use water when it's needed
L itter saves schools
S ave trees.

Poppy Greenough (7)
Hodge Clough Junior School, Oldham

Eco Schools

E nvironment needs help
C lear the environment
O nly use your car when you need it

S ave our planet
C ollect rubbish
H elp recycle
O nly recycle plastic/glass/paper
O nly throw away the rubbish we can't recycle
L ittering is bad.

Ben Holroyd (8)
Hodge Clough Junior School, Oldham

Eco Schools

E co schools
C are about our environment please
O nly use water when you need it

S aving our Earth
C ollecting rubbish
H elp make the environment clean
O nly use lights when needed
O nly use what is needed
L itter do not throw
S ave energy!

Morgan Crossley (8) & Rachael Pollinger (7)
Hodge Clough Junior School, Oldham

Eco Schools

E nergy saving
C omputers turned off
O nly use a bit of electricity

S top throwing chewing gum on the floor
C aring for the environment
H ope for the environment
O nly use black bins
O ld things can be changed into new things
L ight bulbs that save electricity
S ave trees.

Cameron Holland (7) & Elysse Graves (8)
Hodge Clough Junior School, Oldham

Eco Schools

E lectricity gets saved by turning the lights off
C ollecting waste rubbish makes our school tidy
O nly use water when it is needed

S top people from throwing rubbish everywhere
C oming to school on your bike
H elping the environment
O ld tyres can be reused
O r we can recycle them
L ights can be switched off
S ome people say just put your rubbish on the floor.

Victoria Costello (7)
Hodge Clough Junior School, Oldham

Eco Schools

E nergy saving light bulbs
C ompost is food
O ut of cars come fumes

S ave the environment
C omputers switched off saves electricity
H abitats can be saved
O ld food can be recycled
O r reuse plastic bottles
L itter takes a long time to break down
S top people dropping rubbish.

George Crawford (7)
Hodge Clough Junior School, Oldham

Eco Schools

E nergy needs to be saved
C omputers need to be turned off
O nly reuse what needs to be used again

S top using too much energy
C oming to school using your own energy
H elp the world to be a better place
O ld things need to be recycled
O nly recycle the things that are old
L itter needs to be put away
S top making taps drip.

Cameron Whitworth (7)
Hodge Clough Junior School, Oldham

Eco Schools

E nergy saving lights
C ome on and pick up your rubbish
O ld cars can be recycled

S top dropping waste
C ome to school on your scooter
H ave a recycling bin in your garden
O ld tyres can be used with other ones
O nly using what's needed
L itter needs picking up
S top switching the lights on and off.

Joshua Whitehill (7)
Hodge Clough Junior School, Oldham

Eco Schools

E nergy saving light bulb
C ompost, eating and bins
O nly using what's needed

S topping the tap dripping
C oming to school on your bike
H elping the environment to be clean
O ld glass bottles and cans, perhaps we can recycle them
O r we could recycle time and time again
L ights should be switched off when the room is empty
S ome say it's not their problem, but in fact it's all of ours.

Ethan Weeks (7)
Hodge Clough Junior School, Oldham

Eco Schools

E nergy saving light bulbs
C ompost bin needs to be used more
O nly getting things that you need

S top using a lot of paper
C ollecting rubbish
H elping the environment to be clean
O ld things need to be recycled
O r we need to reduce a lot of things
L ights must be switched off
S ome people don't clean up, but they need to.

Amy Shanley (7)
Hodge Clough Junior School, Oldham

Eco Schools

E nergy needs saving
C ollect your rubbish
O ther people don't save their water but they need to

S topping the water when you have used it
C oming to school on your feet or on your bike
H ow about a compost bin?
O ld toys can be used time and time again
O r recycle them
L itter needs picking up
S ome people make other people pick up their rubbish.

Caitlin Feeney (7)
Hodge Clough Junior School, Oldham

Eco Schools

E lectricity needs to be saved
C lose windows and doors
O pen windows and doors when needed

S ave all animals
C are for plants and flowers
H ave safety for animals
O nly use electricity when needed
O n the playground have litter pickers
L ose more gas
S tart recycling more.

Sam Sykes (9)
Hodge Clough Junior School, Oldham

Eco Schools

E lectricity needs to be saved
C omputers turned off after use
O pen windows if needed

S top going in your car
C are for the animals
H elp by recycling paper
O n the playground we have litter pickers
O nly use cars if you have to
L eaving lights on wastes electricity
S ave the school, save the world!

Samuel Biggs (9)
Hodge Clough Junior School, Oldham

Eco Schools

E very day try to walk to school
C lose all windows and doors
O pen windows and doors when needed

S ave all plants and trees
C are for all animals
H ave all local produce
O nly use cars when necessary
O nly use water when needed
L ove our world and look after it
S ave our environment.

John Lord (9)
Hodge Clough Junior School, Oldham

Eco Schools

E lectricity needs to be turned off when not needed
C omputers need to be turned off when not needed
O nly use vehicles when needed

S tart litter picking so the rubbish does not harm animals
C are for the environment
H ave local produce
O nly open windows when needed
O nly have lights on when needed
L ook after plants
S tart walking to school.
   Please start being an eco school!

Alysha Brown (9)
Hodge Clough Junior School, Oldham

Eco Schools

E lectricity must be saved
C arefully make sure you have turned off that computer
O nly use cars when needed

S ave heat, plus keep those windows shut!
C are for animals
H elp them out
O pen windows instead of a fan
O ften try to walk to school
L end a hand by recycling
S tart doing your part *now!*

Morgan Rustidge (10)
Hodge Clough Junior School, Oldham

Eco Schools

E verybody chip in and save electricity
C omputers should be turned off when not in use
O ften check that the lights are turned off

S tart recycling
C are for animals
H ave local produce
O nly use cars when necessary
O n the playground have litter pickers
L ook after our plants
S tart being an eco school!

Hannah Hopkins (10)
Hodge Clough Junior School, Oldham

Eco Schools

E veryone helps save electricity
C areful not to drop litter
O nly use cars for trips

S o turn off computers
C are for animals
H ave milk from nearby farms
O h no, I've dropped litter, pick it up
O pen windows when needed
L ight off at home time
S tart helping!

Kate Matthews (10)
Hodge Clough Junior School, Oldham

Eco Schools

E lectricity should be turned off when not needed
C omputer not used as often
O nly eat organic food

S tart walking to school
C are for plants
H ave local produce
O nly use a bit of heat
O nly use a bit of water
L ights turned off when sunny
S tart recycling now.

Liam Tasker (9)
Hodge Clough Junior School, Oldham

Eco Schools

E lectricity needs to be saved
C areful, computers turned off after use
O ften try to use less electricity

S tart recycling
C are for animals
H elp out to be eco-friendly
O rder local produce
O nly use cars when necessary
L ook after plants
S tart being eco-friendly *now!*

Charmaine Barney (10)
Hodge Clough Junior School, Oldham

Eco Schools

E lectricty needs to be saved
C omputers used only when needed
O nly eat organic food

S ave heat
C are for animals
H ave local produce
O nly open doors and windows when needed
O nly use a little water
L ook after plants and flowers
S ave the environment.

Bryan Pitcher (9)
Hodge Clough Junior School, Oldham

Eco Schools

E lectricity could be saved
C ollect litter
O nly leave taps on when running a bath

S ave electricity
C are for animals
H elp the environment
O nce running a bath, don't fill too high
O nly use cars and vans when needed
L ook after nature
S ave water.

Zac Stansfield (10)
Hodge Clough Junior School, Oldham

Eco Schools

E lectricity needs to be saved
C ut down using lots of electricity
O nly open windows when needed

S ave the plants from dying
C are for animals
H ave local produce
O nly use water when needed
O rganise food
L ook after plants
S tart to pick up litter.

Megan Ashton (10)
Hodge Clough Junior School, Oldham

Eco Schools

E lectricity saving - turn off lights
C lose windows and doors
O nly use cars when necessary

S tart recycling in school
C ars used less in school
H ave local produce
O pen windows only when necessary
O nly use paper when needed
L itter pickers every day
S ave animals that are stuck.

Tia Bell (10)
Hodge Clough Junior School, Oldham

Eco Schools

E nvironment needs to be saved
C omputers turned off after use
O nly use trains when necessary

S tart picking up litter
C ars must save oil
H ave local produce
O n the playground have recycling
O n the playground have bins
L ook after plants and flowers
S ave the world.

Jordan Heywood (10)
Hodge Clough Junior School, Oldham

Eco Schools

E lectricity has to be saved
C heck lights are turned off
O nly use vehicles when necessary

S top heat from escaping
C omputer should be turned off
H ave bins in the playground
O nly use heaters when needed
O nly open windows when necessary
L itter should be picked up
S ave the environment.

Joseph Wharfe (10)
Hodge Clough Junior School, Oldham

Eco Schools

E lectricity needs to be turned off
C omputers use too much electricity
O nly use cars when needed

S tart walking to school
C ars should save oil and gas
H ave local bins
O pen windows and doors if you need to
O n playgrounds people should pick litter up
L ook after plants and flowers
S tart recycling now!

Sascha Langley (9)
Hodge Clough Junior School, Oldham

Eco Schools

E co schools help the environment
C omputers turned off when not in use
O nly use cars when needed

S tart recycling *now!*
C ontinue recycling
H elp the animals
O pen windows only when needed
O n the playground have litter pickers
L ove our world and look after it
S ave the environment.

Thomas Wareing (9)
Hodge Clough Junior School, Oldham

The Busy Days

Saturday, Sunday, a new, fresh day,
Saturday, Sunday, time to do your homework,
Saturday, Sunday, time to play,
Saturday, Sunday, time to cuddle into your bed.

Monday, Tuesday, a new, fresh day,
Monday, Tuesday, time to play,
Monday, Tuesday, time to go home and cheer.

Wednesday, Thursday, a new, fresh day to go to school,
Wednesday, Thursday, time to do PE,
Wednesday, Thursday, time to play,
Wednesday, Thursday, time to go home and have a sleep.

Friday, a new, fresh day to go to school,
Friday, time to play,
Friday, time to go home and have a sleep.

Saturday, Sunday, time to go swimming.

Humairaa Ismail (8)
Lammack Primary School, Blackburn

Autumn

When it is autumn
The leaves twirl and swirl like a bird.
When you step on the leaves
They crackle like a witch laughing at you.
It is like bubbling acid crawling all over you.
When all of the leaves have disappeared
And you can only see the branches,
They look like they are going to crush you
Into bits and bobs.

Khadeejah Abdulla (8)
Lammack Primary School, Blackburn

Vehicles

Vehicles
Are
Fast
Faster than
Fast
Like
A
Lamborghini Gallardo
And
A
Murcilargo.

Vehicles
Are fast
Faster than
Fast
Like
A
Bugatti Veron
That in a race
Can never
Be gone.

Vehicles
Are
Fast
Faster than
Fast
Like
A
Polo
That can
Drive in
Solo.

Vehicles
Are
Fast
Faster than
Fast
That when
You
Run fast
They
Can zoom
Past!

Zain Mathiya (8)
Lammack Primary School, Blackburn

Flowers

Flowers, flowers make the day bright.
Flowers, flowers are full of light.
Flowers, flowers grow in the ground.
Flowers, flowers are sweet and sound.

Aamirah Patel (8)
Lammack Primary School, Blackburn

Cars

Boom, ba, boom! The smoky engine starts
Boom, ba, boom! Buttons light up.
Boom, ba, boom! The car starts.
Boom, ba, boom! The car races.
Boom, ba, boom! Petrol burns up.
Brooooom!

Muhammad Motala (8)
Lammack Primary School, Blackburn

Autumn Days

In autumn the leaves always fall and crumble
They swirl and dance in the sky.

In autumn the trees are as bare as nothing,
Except branches.

In autumn it is a bit cold and chilly.

Amirah Desai (8)
Lammack Primary School, Blackburn

My Brother, Hadees

I crept down the stairs,
Because I heard a dash.
It was my little brother,
He smashed the glass.

Mum came zooming down
And opened the door,
She looked furious
And said, 'No more!'

Tayaab Al-Hassan (8)
Lammack Primary School, Blackburn

My Mum

If a person bullies me,
My mum will always be there.
If I am sad,
My mum will be there.
My mum,
My mum,
My mum.

Farah Musa (8)
Lammack Primary School, Blackburn

Hunger

It sounds like your stomach is asking for food.
It feels like you're never going to eat and you are going to starve.
It reminds me of the people that don't have food.
It looks like everybody has food except me.
It tastes like it's all watery in my mouth.
Hunger is brown, like a volcano erupting.
It smells like freshly baked cake, but I don't get any.

Fatimah Dasu (8)
Lammack Primary School, Blackburn

Silence

Silence looks like a statue still standing there forever.
Silence is as white as the pages of a book.
Silence feels like the ocean swaying side to side.
Silence smells like a daisy swishing in the wind.
Silence reminds me of loneliness.
Silence tastes like fruit growing on the tree.
Silence sounds like no one's about.

Heraa Arif (8)
Lammack Primary School, Blackburn

Hate

Hate is black, like fear.
It feels like bees stinging me on my neck.
It tastes like black blood.
It reminds me of dead animals.
It looks like dinosaurs eating me.
It smells like burning lava.
It sounds like aliens invading.

Ismail Namaji (8)
Lammack Primary School, Blackburn

Don't Get Out Of Your Seat

Don't get out of your seat
Unless you need a pointy, pink pencil.
Don't get out of your seat
Unless you need a blue, blank book.
Don't get out of your seat
Unless you need a pretty, patterned pot.
Don't get out of your seat
Unless you need a real, red rubber.
Don't get out of your seat
Unless you need a shiny, shaky sharpener.
Don't get out of your seat
Unless you need the teacher!

Usaamah Ougradar (8)
Lammack Primary School, Blackburn

School Time

I love school
It's so cool
I like my teachers
When I go out on the playground
I walk all around and about
When school's finished the bell rings
And a phone goes *ting*
I'm so cool and so is school
Ting, ting, there goes the bell
And a phone goes *ring.*

Zaahirah Patel (8)
Lammack Primary School, Blackburn

When We Go To My Nan's House

When we go to my nan's house, my brother sits on the wall,
He thinks he is a cat and he's going to fall,
He's just my brother, Ayhan, watching TV,
But at the same time reminding me of my dad,
He also asks for lemonade,
It smells like fizzy lemon!

When he purrs and miaows,
He sounds like a real live cat,
He curls up in a ball,
Like a sleepy little cat,
He's my cat, no one else can have him.

Asena Akdeniz (8)
Markland Hill Primary School, Bolton

Love

Love is beautiful,
Love is grace,
Love is always suitable,
Love is the greatest place.

Love will always be,
A place for you and me,
Together we will see,
Together we will see.

Love is beautiful,
Love is grace,
Love is always suitable,
Love is the greatest place.

Isobel Tailor (8)
Markland Hill Primary School, Bolton

Laughter

Laughter is bright, sandy orange.
Laughter sounds like the wind blowing.
It tastes like sour oranges tickling the mouth.
Laughter smells like fresh fruit that's just been washed.
It looks like hearts pumping with joy.
Laughter feels like feathers touching the face.
Laughter lives in the fluffy, soft, white clouds of Heaven.

Emma Jo Parr (9)
Markland Hill Primary School, Bolton

Love

Love is bright, shiny pink.
Love is a huge, red heart pumping fast.
It tastes like a sugary sweet in the mouth.
Love smells like a beautiful, shining rose.
It looks like a teddy holding a huge box of chocs.
Love feels as if you are in a beautiful garden.
Love lives in the heart of happiness and can stay forever.

Yunqi Li (8)
Markland Hill Primary School, Bolton

Fun

Fun is bright orange
Fun sounds like a noisy fair
It tastes like fizzy orange juice
Fun smells like ripe fruit
It looks like a happy, sunny day
Fun lives in the sun.

William Gorman (9)
Markland Hill Primary School, Bolton

Beauty

Beauty is a pink rose
Beauty sounds like wedding bells on a wedding day
It tastes like a gorgeous strawberry
Beauty smells like flowers
It looks like a pink rose
Beauty lives in a make-up box.

Molly Magee (9)
Markland Hill Primary School, Bolton

Death

Death is dark black
Death sounds like eternal silence
It tastes like deep black
Death smells like burning flesh
It looks like a reaper
Death feels like cold rock
Death lives in the fabric of Hell.

James Whalley (9)
Markland Hill Primary School, Bolton

Fun

Fun is bright yellow
Fun sounds like laughing babies
It tastes like sweets
Fun smells like lavender
It looks like a rose
Fun feels like soft teddies
Fun lives in children.

Thomas Cummins (9)
Markland Hill Primary School, Bolton

Fun

Fun is a shocking, golden yellow
Fun is the sound of happy kids
It has a sweet, bubbly flavour which fizzes through your body
Fun smells pure and rich
It looks like the cork of a champagne bottle popping off with joy
Fun feels warm and bendy
Fun lives in the soul of a child!

Alice Entwistle (9)
Markland Hill Primary School, Bolton

Beauty

Beauty is the colour of the sunset,
It sounds like the sea crashing,
Beauty tastes like chocolate melting,
It smells like pretty red roses,
Beauty looks like the sun,
Beauty feels like soft baby skin,
Beauty lives in the heart of the ocean!

Millie Dawson (9)
Markland Hill Primary School, Bolton

Death

Death is a darkened black
Death sounds like a sword meeting flesh
It tastes like water as it meets blood
Death smells like hard flesh from bones
It looks like a black cloak from Hell
Death feels like black ice on your teeth
Death lives within.

Calum Smith (9)
Markland Hill Primary School, Bolton

Death

Death is black
It sounds like people screaming in terror
Death tastes like blood crashing
It smells like wood burning
It looks like new red and black shoes
Death feels like a scorpion nipping me
Death lives in Hell.

Luke Charnock (9)
Markland Hill Primary School, Bolton

Happiness

Happiness is light, shiny yellow
Happiness sounds like happy children
It tastes like lemon lollies and sour sherbet
Happiness smells like lovely flowers
It looks like a smiling sun
Happiness feels like fluffy bunnies
Happiness lives in the heart of joy.

Myles Crofts (9)
Markland Hill Primary School, Bolton

Fun

Fun is happy, red and shiny
Fun sounds like fizzy orange
It tastes like happiness
It looks like a burning sun
Fun feels like chewing gum
Fun lives in the heart
Fun is a cool dude.

Matthew Bates (9)
Markland Hill Primary School, Bolton

Beauty

Beauty is the colour of pastel, prancing pink.
Beauty sounds like people eating chocolate Crunchie bars.
It tastes like dark chocolate that has just been melted.
Beauty smells like chocolate flavoured lipgloss.
It looks like pretty pastel pink fireworks.
Beauty lives in my heart!

Sarah Minney (9)
Markland Hill Primary School, Bolton

Beauty

Beauty is baby pink,
It sounds like wedding bells,
It tastes like pink tropical juice on a hot, sunny day.
It smells like fresh nail varnish.
It looks like a glossy rose.
It feels like baby's soft cheeks.
Beauty lives in a crowded make-up box.

Elizabeth Wood (9)
Markland Hill Primary School, Bolton

Darkness

Darkness is an empty void.
Darkness sounds like a group of screams.
Darkness tastes like a scary bite.
Darkness smells like a brain-jamming smell.
It looks like a terrifying sight.
It lives in the deepest, darkest dungeon.
It feels like Dracula's teeth!

Mohammed Nadat (8)
Markland Hill Primary School, Bolton

Anger

Anger is red like a fierce bomb about to explode in your head.
It tastes like old, green, burnt bread.
It sounds like an animal being tested.
It smells like being infested by bugs.
It looks like a red tomato about to be eaten.
It feels like a smelly, old foot.
It reminds me of *anger!*

Jack Bannister (8)
Markland Hill Primary School, Bolton

Happiness

Happiness is the smile of life
It sounds like someone is pleading out with joy
It tastes like 100 Haribos in your mouth
It smells like a piece of chocolate
And it feels like a cuddly, fluffy teddy
Happiness reminds me of my mum when she's happy with joy!

Sam Hassall (8)
Markland Hill Primary School, Bolton

Anger

Anger is terrible, anger is fire
Anger is the sound of a volcano
Anger is red and people like red
Anger is red like the Teletubbie, Po.

Anger is red, so don't get mad
Anger is red, so don't eat a tomato
Anger is red, so don't go red in the face
Anger is red, so do not hurt yourself.

Ghalib Hashmi (9)
Markland Hill Primary School, Bolton

Loneliness

Shining, grey pools of moonlight
Reflect no other reflection but your own.
Unbearable, cold custard oozing down your throat.
Stale bread creeps around your nostrils.
A wilderness with only a rock for comfort.
The beating of your own heart
And the gasping of your own breath.
Cold ice slowly clasping your body.

Julia Sabery (11)
Markland Hill Primary School, Bolton

Deceit

Deceit is black, dreadful and devious,
Poisoned rice pudding chugging down your throat,
Stinking of deadly smoke lurking in your nose,
A bat that just returned from the depths of Hell,
Just like a monkey screeching for help,
Formed as a cold stone weighing you down.
This is Deceit!

Alexandra Darbyshire (10)
Markland Hill Primary School, Bolton

Depression

Blue, icy water,
Soggy crisps in your mouth,
Mouldy cheese circles your nose,
Guts pop before your eyes,
Screeching violins all around you,
Spiky nettles meet your fingers.

Scott Corrigan (10)
Markland Hill Primary School, Bolton

Beauty

Beauty is pure pale white.
It sounds like a cool breeze.
Beauty tastes like cold spring water.
It smells like a new spring snowdrop.
Beauty looks like a young lady in a white coat.
It feels like a soft silk cushion.
Beauty lives in a sunny part of heaven.

Rebecca Vincent (8)
Markland Hill Primary School, Bolton

Death

Death is as dark black as a stormy cloud.
Death sounds like silence at a funeral.
It tastes like burnt toast.
Death smells like oil in the wreck of a car.
It looks like smoke from a shotgun.
Death feels like plain nothing.
Death lives in the clouds of Hell!

Gracelyn Byrne (9)
Markland Hill Primary School, Bolton

Silence

Silence is blank white.
Silence sounds like empty mouths.
It tastes bland and numb in your mouth.
Silence smells of fresh air.
It looks like a new, fresh whiteboard.
Silence feels like nothing.
Silence lives in you.

Eleanor Goulding (9)
Markland Hill Primary School, Bolton

Anger

Anger is in the room,
Anger is in a tomb,
Anger is as red as a fire,
Anger is as long as a wire.

Anger is everywhere,
Anger is in the air,
Anger is very strong,
Anger comes out of your tongue.

Anger works in your body,
Anger works on a boy called Nody,
Anger is everywhere,
Anger is in the air.

Heather Walton (9)
Markland Hill Primary School, Bolton

Love

Love is beautiful
Love is great
Love has happiness
In every way
It always makes my day
It happens to be the right way

Love is beautiful
Love is great
Love is like the world
To me and you
So what shall we do?

Jessica Dhodakia (9)
Markland Hill Primary School, Bolton

Darkness In The Night

It's as cold as ice
And forces you to eat mice.
Its sounds are piercing through your ear
And starting to bring you fear.
When the rain starts to pour
You go into the graveyard and start to draw.

It tastes like paint in an apple
As you walk into a chapel.
It feels as cold as wind
And then there was a letter pinned
To the wall!

Elizabeth Waudby (9)
Markland Hill Primary School, Bolton

Anger

Anger is fierce
It sounds like an exploding volcano
It tastes like chilli
It smells like horror
It looks like a red tomato
It feels mad
It reminds me of a cross giant!

Anger is like a charging elephant
It sounds like a spooky place
It tastes like a horrible tomato
It smells like a raw carrot
It looks like a very red apple
It feels like a horrible wind
It reminds me of a dinosaur!

Aimee Parr (7)
Markland Hill Primary School, Bolton

Darkness

Darkness is a pitch-black drift floating in the night,
It tastes very bitter at the same time very sweet,
It sounds like a howling wolf screaming out of sight,
It smells like very, very rotten meat.
It looks like a monster that makes you want to scream,
It feels like you have been hit by something big,
It reminds me of a ghost that is never seen.

Edward Fisher (8)
Markland Hill Primary School, Bolton

Anger

Anger is red, full of aggression,
A bowl of rotten soup stalking your mouth,
A cup of salty water following your nose,
Black, stormy clouds appearing wherever you go,
Thunder and lightning clashing outside your house,
Putting your hand into a kettle while it's boiling.

Hassan Baz (11)
Markland Hill Primary School, Bolton

Happiness

Pink balloons bundled with joy,
A burst of fluffy candyfloss alive with flavour,
The scent of fresh roses on a summer's day,
The first steps of paradise is laid before your eyes,
Singing birds entertaining on the rooftops,
A soft kitten's fur purring in your hands.

Khadija Amla (10)
Markland Hill Primary School, Bolton

Loneliness

Grey, plain, rough rocks,
Sour, cold milk trickling slowly off your tongue,
A distant empty smell of smoke wanders around your nose,
The dark midnight sky, all cold and frosty, encircles your vision,
Silence, quiet and alone, echoes into your ears,
Salty, watery tears prickle your cheeks.
You are alone.

Leila Safi (11)
Markland Hill Primary School, Bolton

Anger

Red, darker than the Devil.
Burning potatoes scald your throat.
Cold mustard stalks your nostrils.
Treacherous Hell taunts your dreams.
Painful screams haunt your ears.
A cold, lonely room surrounds you.
You are alone.
Anger has chosen you as its next victim!

Muhammad Karim (11)
Markland Hill Primary School, Bolton

Anger

Black, the colour of Hell,
Blood, slithering down your throat,
Rotten cheese hovering around,
A crackling fire surrounding you,
People screaming before their death,
Slimy, black jelly covering your body.

Nathan Dhodakia (11)
Markland Hill Primary School, Bolton

Jealousy

Green; poisonous ivy crawling up your body,
Bitter lemons force themselves down your throat,
The scent of sick drifts around your nose,
An abandoned house, bare and unpleasant, fills your field of vision,
Fingernails scraping down a blackboard brings beastly music to
your ears,
A porcupine's spike pierces into your skin. *Ouch!*

Ellie McGivern (10)
Markland Hill Primary School, Bolton

Happiness

Yellow; sunshine peering through the clouds,
Hot chocolate trickling through your body,
Sweet hyacinths fill your nose with wonderful spices,
A never-ending field of beautiful tulips,
Birds singing in the trees outside your window,
A soft, fluffy cushion to keep you warm on a cold winter's day.

Eleanor Schenk (11)
Markland Hill Primary School, Bolton

Jealousy

Jealousy is green, raging inside you,
Chilli powder burns your mouth,
The smell of rotten eggs lingers around you,
A face stares at you, not blinking or moving,
Wolves howling, never stopping,
Ice freezes your fingertips,
Jealousy.

Jennifer Walmsley (11)
Markland Hill Primary School, Bolton

Love

Pink; spring blossom,
Melting candyfloss trickling against your taste buds,
A scent of juicy apricots hovers in your nose,
A whole new world fills your vision,
Sounds like a herd of doves, filling your ears,
Sand slipping around your fingertips.

Charlotte Bannister (11)
Markland Hill Primary School, Bolton

Darkness

Darkness sweeps round your room at night
Whilst you're cuddled up tight.
You really hate it
And it gives you a really, really terrible fright.
So you cuddle up tighter,
But then you hear a sound,
You think it's your mum,
But it's just a rider.
But then you wake up
And the day is dawning
And soon you find it's morning.

Ross Tracey (9)
Markland Hill Primary School, Bolton

Joy!

Yellow; the sun shining down on Earth,
Chocolate dribbling down your chin,
Bread, fresh out of the oven,
Animals joyfully playing in the wilderness,
Birds bursting into song,
Holding a cute puppy.

Bradley Light (11)
Markland Hill Primary School, Bolton

Darkness

Darkness is black, like a black giant invading the Earth,
The stars twinkle in the air like light on a baby's birth,
When the sun sets, the world becomes dark,
The colours are blue, pink and orange, like some colours from a park.

When the clock strikes twelve, it turns midnight,
If there's a shooting star, it'll make things bright.
If you walk in the dark, you'll need a torch to see,
It's so dark that you'd better be careful because you might get stung
by a bee.

Feeling dark is feeling the air,
Dark also looks like a person with dark hair.

Priya Guhathakurta (7)
Markland Hill Primary School, Bolton

Anger

Anger is red, like a burning fire,
Red blood gushing through bodies,
People red in the face,
Is it embarrassment? No anger!
Smells like fire burning near,
Tastes like smoke high in the sky.
It looks like a pretty, fiery glow,
It feels hot, just like anger,
It reminds me of when my mum gets mad.

Thomas Mair (8)
Markland Hill Primary School, Bolton

Love

A bunch of red roses,
Warm jam running freely down your throat,
A wonderful garden bursting with wild flowers,
Valentine's Days fill your body with red, beating hearts,
A silky dressing gown enchants your fingers . . .
Love.

Megan Halsall (10)
Markland Hill Primary School, Bolton

Excitement

One million shocking pink balloons float across your eyes,
Zingy oranges and lemons test your taste buds,
The aroma of fresh washing dances in the breeze,
Bubbles drift into your line of vision, popping at every instant,
Screaming children blast down your ear,
Fingers tickle every part of your body.

Lucy Entwistle (10)
Markland Hill Primary School, Bolton

The Dog In The Winter

In winter when frost froze the house,
The pet dog howled outside,
Like the wind and
Chewed its bone like a cheetah,
Cold as a freezer, it went home!

Dan Green (7)
Nateby Primary School, Preston

Scary Dreams

Sometimes dreams are scary,
Very scary,
Sometimes ghosts, skeletons,
Boo!
Sometimes squeaky rats -
People crying,
Sometimes these things happen in my dreams,
Sometimes dreams are like black clouds in the sky,
They are *nightmares!*

Abbie Hewitt (7)
Nateby Primary School, Preston

Pet On Holiday

I have a pet - a hairy pet - called *Hairy Mary!*
I took my pet on holiday,
It was very scary,
She growled and jumped, then ran away,
I cried and cried all day,
'Woof, woof,' she jumped up on my bed,
'Don't do that again,' I said.

Faye Taylor-McCormick (8)
Nateby Primary School, Preston

Holidays

Sunny, sunny Spain,
Children splashing - happy,
Happy in the pool,
Children building sandcastles,
Soft, soft, sand,
Holidays are over until next year,
Sunny, sunny Spain.

Josh Mitchell (7)
Nateby Primary School, Preston

Animals

The kangaroo's jumping like a slinky,
Stepping on all of the ants beneath him,
The insects scurry like rockets,
Elephants smacking down trees,
Like a bulldozer crushing down trees,
At home, cat's pouncing from side to side,
Jumping from table to table,
Leaping from chair to chair,
Dogs give an ear-piercing growl.

Sam Collinson (8)
Nateby Primary School, Preston

Pets

Pets can be big or small,
Pets can be good or bad,
Pets can be trained or not trained,
I have big pets and small pets,
I have good pets and bad pets,
I have pets that are trained and not trained,
My best pet is my chicken.

Freddie Hewitt (9)
Nateby Primary School, Preston

My Horse Rocky

Rocky is a black cob,
Rocky is three years old,
His mane is as black as oil,
A flash of white on his feet like paper,
Lots of hair and fluff,
At the bottom of his feet.

Chloe May Illingworth (7)
Nateby Primary School, Preston

Pets And Other Animals

At home -
Some pets are big,
Some pets are small,
Some pets are short, some pets are tall.
Don't you hear the dog barking at the door?
There are fish swimming like a shark,
In the bowl.

In the sea -
Crabs scuttle down in the sand,
Like a fork tapping on a plate at tea.

In the jungle -
The lion with its great big roar,
As loud as an alarm bell prowling around.

Olivia Barlow (8)
Nateby Primary School, Preston

School

School is fun, fun, fun,
School is good, good, good,
Playing in the playground in the best,
Yum, yum, yum hot chocolate,
Playing spies with Josh, Dan, Robert, James,
Ring, ring! It's time to go in.

Finlay Bracken (7)
Nateby Primary School, Preston

Holidays

The seas are as blue as the sky,
The sun is a bright burning ball,
The dolphins are leaping in and out of the water,
We are building sandcastles,
People are having picnics by the sea,
Toddlers are paddling,
Teenagers are sunbathing.

Later

The golden sand sparkles in the moonlight,
The rocks are grey as clay,
The moon is white as snow,
The fish are sleeping down in the deep blue sea,
Seals are falling to sleep on the rocks.

Alice Danson (8)
Nateby Primary School, Preston

Holidays

I go on the beach,
Sand is scorching like a bonfire,
Sand dunes as spiky as puffer fish,
Seagulls swooping and swooping for fish,
Ice cream vans,
Hot dogs as delicious as can be,
Fish wriggle in the water,
Boats as wrecked as a landfill.

Robert Slater (7)
Nateby Primary School, Preston

Dreams

One night, I fell asleep,
I had a lovely dream,
A fantastic dream!
Dogs, frogs, cats and bats all in separate rooms,
'Squeak' just like a mouse - *'Squeak'*
A mouse as small as a pea,
What such a funny sight to see.

Next morning when I awoke,
On my bed a cat!
Hanging from my curtain pole was a bat,
What next? *'Croak'* - *'Croak!'* oh no! Not a frog,
But no dog there was,
My dream was alive but no dog oh no!
No bark, no woof, no dark brown fur,
I saw a tiny something right on the end of my nose,
As small as a pea, as white as a ghost,
Out of my dream came the mouse,
But still no dog!
A cat, a mouse and a frog,
What was that I heard?
Barking - surely not.

Then I saw it, it looked poorly,
It had dark brown fur,
Next I heard a woof, a bark,
Now my dreams had come to life!

Harriet Kelsall (8)
Nateby Primary School, Preston

Holidays

Go on holiday, it is lovely,
On the beach, don't forget,
Laugh with the people that you have met,
Exciting holidays are the best,
If you have invited a guest.

Rachel Bell (9)
Nateby Primary School, Preston

Mad Pets

Mum's gone to the shops!
'Look after the pets,' she warned,
I'm watching TV,
The pets are howling like roaring fires,
The dogs want a walk,
Cat Chloe got out the gate,
Rabbit's gone mad,
Tortoise is asleep, looks like a dead mouse,
The fish have got a disease,
Guinea pigs running around the garden,
Peregrine falcon firing down,
I go upstairs to see where Mum is,
Oh dear! Mum's nearly back,
I get pets in cages,
All pets in cages - done,
Oh no! Cat Chloe's still out,
I got her in the house,
Mum just got back,
'Good work, here is £5.00,' she says,
'Phew!'

Peter Walton (9)
Nateby Primary School, Preston

Best Friends

Girls are playing together,
Everybody will see,
What you can be,
When you have a friend,
Your friendship won't come to an end,
Eating, drinking smoothies, sleeping over,
It's good fun,
What is best is:
Your friendship won't come to an end.

Eleanor Moss (8)
Nateby Primary School, Preston

Pets

The dogs are as loud as a wagon,
Dogs chase the cats,
'Stop it, Charlie stop chasing the cats,'
Ordered Mrs Parker!
Now the dogs and cats are as quiet as a mouse,
Rabbits rustling and hamsters squeaking like guinea pigs,
Hear the horse neighing in the field next door,
Like a lullaby saying *goodnight,*
'Come on Sunshine - to the paddock to ride,'
Said Mrs Parker's daughter,
Clip, clop, clip, clop went Sunshine's feet like castanets.

Hannah Lawrenson (8)
Nateby Primary School, Preston

Holidays

I went on holiday,
The sun was roaring like a fire,
The swimming pool felt as cold as winter rain,
Went down to where people were having picnics,
People running away from howling waves,
But some people dive into the waves
And swim in the choppy sea,
Most people buy ice creams and eat them in the sun,
Happy holidays!

James Davis (8)
Nateby Primary School, Preston

Lent

L ent is when Jesus was crucified,
E aster is when all new beginning's happen,
N ature is wildlife's place,
T housand years from now people will understand Jesus.

Jade Mashiter (8)
Overton St Helen's CE School, Overton

Mum

You're the new sparkling leaf being turned over,
You are the taste of apple juice on my tongue,
You are the new sun shining in the glistening sky,
You are the smell of fresh air in the sky,
You are the smell of newly toasted bread.

Tom Morbey (8)
Overton St Helen's CE School, Overton

Dad

You're the light blue sky in the day,
You're my piece of cake for my treat,
You're my best pop band in the world,
You're like my pet penguin,
Sliding through the snow,
You're like a bottle of Coke for my drink,
You're my best place Nandos,
You're like when I get my maths right in my book,
You're the water coming out of the tap.

Natalie Mason-Brown (9)
Overton St Helen's CE School, Overton

Cat In The Window

Cat in the window,
What can you see?
A dog barking in the park,
A bird flying in the sky singing,
Some cats miaowing,
A bunny jumping,
Glass being broken.

Aimee Bailey (8)
Overton St Helen's CE School, Overton

The Magic Box
(Inspired by 'Magic Box' by Kit Wright)

I will put in the box,
The sunrise in the sky turning from pink to orange,
The yellow sun shining on the beach,
And the first snowball.

I will put in the box . . .
The dream of touching the sky,
The smell of food in the frying pan,
And the feeling of a tight hug from my mum.

The box is decorated with lion's teeth on the corners,
And the brown twigs from a cut tree on the sides.

I will put in the box . . .
A dream of being the tallest in the world,
A feeling of kisses from my dad,
And the smell of petrol at the garage.

I will put in the box . . .
A smell of chips at a chip shop,
A dog chasing a cat down the road,
And a man taking bins away.

Eve Abdel Moneim (8)
Overton St Helen's CE School, Overton

My Brother Max

You are a new laid sun,
Flying a thousand light years away,
With a glistening blue sky around you,
You are the rap,
That never gets worse,
You are the squeezed orange,
That has been squeezed to orange juice,
You are the orange bit of a melon,
That I love so much.

George Higginson (8)
Overton St Helen's CE School, Overton

The Magic Box
(Inspired by 'Magic Box' by Kit Wright)

I will put in the box . . .
The buttons of a TV remote,
The fur of a cat's coat,
A piece of shiny wood,
Cut from a bridge.

I will put in the box . . .
The feel of the sun,
As it touches my skin,
The fizziness of Coke,
As it touches my tongue,
A piece of silk,
From my bed cover.

My box is fastened,
With a wave of the sea,
A shooting star,
Stuck to the lid,
Clay shaped as stars,
As the wood of the box.

Grace Abdel Moneim (8)
Overton St Helen's CE School, Overton

The Magic Box
(Inspired by 'Magic Box' by Kit Wright)

I will put in the box . . .
A key to a world of luxury,
The moon and stars so close to me,
The dream of jumping on the clouds,
Chocolate mountain ready to erupt,
The smell of fresh air drifting,
The hot sun all over me.

Roger Mall (8)
Overton St Helen's CE School, Overton

The Magic Box
(Inspired by 'Magic Box' by Kit Wright)

I will put in the box of treasure . . .
The smell of melted chocolate,
The key to a magical world.

I will put in the box . . .
Lots of different toys,
The sound of music far away,
The look of the sun going down for the night,
The dream of being an artist,
The key to an endless passage,
A door to Heaven.

My box is made out of wood with carvings of metal,
Rectangles for a stand with heads and snakes carved on,
It has dinosaur's toes for hinges,
A snake guarding the key,
There are lots of secrets to get into it.

Wilk Morbey (8)
Overton St Helen's CE School, Overton

Alfie

Alfie is like . . .

My teddy bear when I snuggle up to him,
His cute face is like the sun going down,
At the end of the day,
He makes my heart pump faster,
When I see his face,
When he runs through the fields,
You cannot see him because he is camouflaged,
He is my best pet ever,
That is why I like my dog.

Oliver Whitehead (9)
Overton St Helen's CE School, Overton

The Magic Box
(Inspired by 'Magic Box' by Kit Wright)

I will put in the box . . .
A dream about riding a unicorn,
The taste of chocolate melting in a bowl,
The fresh taste of chips,
A key to the door of an imaginary world,
A frog leaping across lily pads,
The smell of a beautiful rose,
A fresh apple growing on the tree,
The smell of fresh vegetables,
The sound of milk pouring,
A ruby twinkling in a jewellery shop,
The stars twinkling in the sky,
Milk pouring from a cow's udder.

My box is glittered with stars and jewels,
Silk covered in the corners.

My box is made of steel,
Stars in the corners,
Secrets all over my box.

Lily Fegan (8)
Overton St Helen's CE School, Overton

A Cat Called Angel

Her ears are pointed up like daffodils,
Her feet patter like a little mouse,
Her face is so fluffy and soft,
Her tail sways like a flower in the wind,
She is like a little fairy,
Her eyes glow in the dark like two fireflies,
Her back is furry and smooth,
Her whiskers are pointed like thin stems from a flower,
Angel is the best cat in the world.

Anna Hebblewhite (8)
Overton St Helen's CE School, Overton

Ping Pong

Ping Pong is a monster,
I made up last week,
A monster so scary,
I'm now losing sleep.

It has . . .
A giant spider as its head,
Two mouldy sprouts as eyes,
One hundred red ants as its nose,
Worms and slugs as hair,
Green slimy goo as its tongue.

Down to its body, it has . . .
Slimy, slithery eels ready to bite,
Snakeskin stuck to its tummy,
Gigantic spikes for its legs,
Rotten mushrooms for its feet.

Ping Pong is my monster,
I made up in my mind,
If you look there for monsters,
Beware what you find!

Hannah Jackson (9)
Overton St Helen's CE School, Overton

Mum

You are a red rose,
You are the black horses,
Gleaming in a field,
You sing like High School Musical,
You are a plate of fish and chips,
You are the ticks in my maths book.

Kathryn Barrett (8)
Overton St Helen's CE School, Overton

The Magic Box
(Inspired by 'Magic Box' by Kit Wright)

I will put in the box . . .
The golden sunrise on a summer's morning,
The sea whooshing against the rocks,
The smell of newly cut grass,
The taste of heated chocolate melting on my tongue,
The sound of birds whistling in the morning sun,
The smell of newly made cakes cooking in the oven,
The sound of my sister laughing, so loud.

My box is made of wood and gems,
With sparkly sequins on the top,
And inside there is lovely, soft fluff,
To keep my favourite things inside.

Rebecca Wakefield (9)
Overton St Helen's CE School, Overton

My Mum

You're blue like the waves,
Filling up the sea,
Your hand is like silk,
Rubbing against me,
You're like chocolate,
And sweets too,
And I always feel better,
When talking to you,
You are hot chocolate,
Touching my face,
You are home,
My favourite place,
And you're just my favourite song,
Shine, by *Take That,*
And we both sing along.

Jaimie O'Brien (9)
Overton St Helen's CE School, Overton

When I Grow Up

When I grow up,
I want to be a scientist.
Earn a million,
Earn a billion,
Make a cure for all illnesses,
And have shelves of ingredients.

I will invent a time machine,
And travel to the future,
See an alien,
Make a new species,
Go a thousand miles away.

When I grow up,
I want to be an artist,
Earn a million,
Earn a billion,
Create something wondrous,
And be so famous.

George Higginson (8)
Overton St Helen's CE School, Overton

Anna

You are a red tulip just grown,
Golden chips just put in the oven,
Gorgeous smooth silk across my headboard,
You are Coca-Cola just poured,
In a lovely smooth glass,
You are there for me when I am hurt,
And you warm my heart,
You are the grass swaying in my garden,
And you are the pizza sauce just spread.

Marnie Cvetkovic-Jones (8)
Overton St Helen's CE School, Overton

Nee

Nee you're like a rose,
And a starfish tingling me,
You're like silk going down my arm,
And you're like the smell of herbs,
You are like the silver stars in the sky,
You're like a cat purring every night on the wall,
Your life is mine.

Amelia Glackin-Melici (7)
Overton St Helen's CE School, Overton

Lily

You're like the sun in the sky,
You're like a new rose in the breeze,
Your hair is like fresh caramel,
Your skin is like orange juice,
You're fresh as chips,
Your skin is like milk.

Kelsey Hadwin (9)
Overton St Helen's CE School, Overton

Cat In The Window

Cat in the window,
What do you see?
A bird chirping from a tree,
Rain pattering from the roofs,
Horses stamping with their hooves,
The rain gurgling as rain drips,
The girl screaming as she trips,
The wind tossing leaves about,
The boy sulking because he wants to go out.

Jaimie O'Brien (9)
Overton St Helen's CE School, Overton

My Feelings Inside And Around Me

There are many things I'd like to say about my life, my life today,
The feel of the fresh air coming through the window,
The bright sun shining on a day that's new,
I can hear cars zooming by like cheetahs galloping by.

Children playing like it's a funfair,
Making sandcastles trying to reach the air,
Insects, humans all in the shadow, not to get burnt every time,
The ladies smell of lovely perfume coming with the
                              breeze to my room.

I can smell that barbecue food all the time,
Neighbours eating scrumptious meals,
Just smell that lovely food,
Kitchen pots and pans are smashing by the boiling sun.

Everybody's in the house in the evening,
The day goes by really quickly,
Children are waiting for the next day to start,
So they can have the fun to start again.

Samra Shahbaz (11)
St Agnes CE Primary School, Longsight

Sadness

I look outside my window and
I can see the sky blue,
It makes me feel quite sad inside,
It makes me feel quite blue,
I can hear the silence of my own sound,
I can see the sadness around me,
All this sadness fills my head,
The sadness which comes down upon my bed,
Fresh air does not help my sadness,
It can't make it go away,
Some things might come into my life and maybe
One day my sadness will go away!

Fahad Hussain (10)
St Agnes CE Primary School, Longsight

Home Sweet Home

I go home after school,
To take a shower,
But to my surprise I find it taken,
By my smelly old brother.

Instead I go downstairs,
Wanting to watch TV,
But then again, bad idea,
As my stupid sister won't let me.

I then decided to go in the kitchen,
To find some food,
But that's not going to happen
As my mum's late from work
And in a right old mood.

So I went in my room,
To start the computer,
But Dad's there, painting the walls,
In a gruesome grey colour.

So you see, home is not a place,
Where I would like to be,
I can't even pop to the toilets,
To take a wee!

I would like to be in a different place,
A place like Rome,
But I'm stuck here,
Home sweet home.

Sadia Khan (9)
St Agnes CE Primary School, Longsight

Changes

Happiness, sadness, fear and hope are all the things I have
Dangling from my rope,
I look outside my window and see,
Fighting and grabbing and it hurts me inside shockingly.

Ice-cold wind with continuous rain,
Little splashes falling swiftly on my windowpane,
I felt a mysterious pain in my head,
I couldn't control it so I lay in my bed.

I keep on thinking about my home,
Thinking, thinking, about my family and friends,
Because I love them so much,
While sitting on my bed all alone.

I hate my life, I really do,
There are other people in the world just like me too,
Some are luckier than I am, some aren't,
At least I know my family will be with me for evermore.

Delwar Kabir (10)
St Agnes CE Primary School, Longsight

My Poem

Happiness and sadness, fear and hope
Are all dangling round my rope,
I stare at everything I see with my fierce rope,
After that I feel lonely and run up my red rope.

When I look out my window,
I can see the sky, which makes me feel quite blue,
When rains it makes me feel furious and
Makes me think of other people.

When I look out my window, I feel glad that the sun is out
And I can see all the flowers blowing away and
I can see the wind blowing all the bees away.

Ahsan Anwar (10)
St Agnes CE Primary School, Longsight

My School

Oh how I love my school and when the wind blows in my hair
Or when my teachers love and care,
When my teachers shout at us, they really don't mean it in a bad way,
And when they glare at us, it is just a way to tell the students
Not to be naughty.

When it is dinner time and as we run and play,
We can always feel our heart beating,
The day the school is going to get knocked down,
I will feel sad and will not learn anything.

The day I went home, my head was down and
I was full of tears, I locked myself in my room,
Thinking how the new school is going to be like.

Bilal Imran (10)
St Agnes CE Primary School, Longsight

What Do I See?

I look outside my window,
What do I see?
Birds up in the sky flying high towards the
Sunrise shooting through my window.

I don't know what to say about me and my life,
So tell me what do I say?
I say I see children having fun,
Some adults shouting, their voices echoing,
Cars, vans on the road driving through the rush hour,
The smell of perfume surrounding me and the
Smell of flowers in my mind,
I say, I see, I hear something or someone creeping up,
Me and my heart getting terrified and who should it be . . .
My brother.

Maaria Ahmad (10)
St Agnes CE Primary School, Longsight

The Poem Of My Life!

There are a thousand things,
Hanging from my rope,
That are filled with joy, fear and hope.

One of the things I'd like to say is:
Is about my life today,
I mostly feel happy because of my friends,
I'm impressed because they will be with me till time ends.

When I look out of my window,
I see huge buildings and great big clouds,
That look like candyfloss,
I also see girls and boys playing a fun game of toss.

When I turn on my music,
And listen to the melody,
I hear bees buzzing and birds singing,
I also hear school bells jingling and jingling.

Whenever I walk into my mum's kitchen,
I smell her lovely cooking,
And outside I smell pollution and smoke,
Also my sister's perfume of oak.

This is the end of my thoughts and themes,
I still look in the sky and see the magical sunbeam,
All of the thoughts that have been said today,
Are worth to say!

Sabah Afzal (11)
St Agnes CE Primary School, Longsight

Casual Poem

Happiness, broken-hearted,
Horror and hope,
Are all the thoughts,
I have dangling on my rope!

The feelings I have are very melancholy
And some of my feelings are filled with ecstasy.

The things I see around my life are birds,
Children playing, cars
And I can see people smoking tars.

The things I smell around my life
Are people making and baking,
It smells like they just baked a cake.

The things I hear around my life
Are people talking, birds twitting
And children humming.

I am feeling very bored,
Nobody telling me to play,
I wish someone did say this phrase today.

Sadikur Rahman (10)
St Agnes CE Primary School, Longsight

I Dreamt I Was Riding A Zebra

I dreamt I was riding a zebra,
With curly pink hair on my head,
Then I woke up that morning,
That zebra was on my bed.

I rode into school on my zebra,
It caused all the teachers to scream,
But then I was slightly embarrassed,
To find it was still a dream.

I woke up again in my bedroom,
And saw with relief and a laugh,
I don't have a pink-headed zebra,
I guess I'll just ride the giraffe.

Maria Stokes (10)
St Agnes CE Primary School, Longsight

Feelings

Happiness, sadness, fear and hope,
Are all the thoughts I have hanging on my rope,
I'd like to share many things with you,
And spread them out like a bird's wings
Because I can trust you.

The sun shining and glittering,
Just makes me want to dance and sing,
The sparkling moon comes out at night,
Making the darkness, very, very bright.

I wake up in the morning and fly out of my bed,
To open the curtains and to show the whole wide world
To my little bear, Ted.

I wonder what will happen for every minute of today,
But I do know I am going to try and do things my way.

Yasmina Akhter (10)
St Agnes CE Primary School, Longsight

Friendship

Friends keep you happy,
Friends make you smile,
They walk with you through every mile,
They make you laugh and giggle,
Even by the smallest tickle,
Friends are always there,
Promises they share,
Friends who make sure you have fun,
They play games, jump, skip and run,
Friends are very caring,
And also always sharing.

Aliyah Begum (9)
St Agnes CE Primary School, Longsight

Happiness

I look outside my window and I see the sun shining,
It makes me feel happy because I like the sun so much!

I look outside my window and see the snowfall,
I see snowmen being built in the lovely winter snow!

I look outside my window and see the lovely flowers,
They make me feel so happy because they look so pretty!

I look outside my window and I see the autumn leaves,
They make me feel so happy because I love the autumn breeze!

Habib Tajwar (10)
St Agnes CE Primary School, Longsight

Best Friends!

My friends are my best friends,
The best friends in the world,
They keep promises and share secrets
Anytime they want too,
If they fall or hurt, I go and help them every day.

We will always stick together even
If one of them is feeling blue,
Therefore we will stay as friends,
Every single day!

Amina Rahman (10)
St Agnes CE Primary School, Longsight

Hamster

A vegetable eater,
A snoring sleeper,
A human biter,
A night player,
A food storer,
A little lighter,
A water sucker,
A fast runner,
A small escaper,
A day sleeper,
A strong pusher,
A little listener,
A little nibbler,
A ground stayer,
A little smeller,
A little climber.

Morgan Robinson (8)
St James' CE Primary School, Clitheroe

Leopards

A spotty hunter,
A fast runner,
A meat eater,
A fast high jumper,
A quick good hibernator,
An agile swimmer,
A man eater,
A kind loving creature,
A cold hater,
A warm hugger,
An eye gleamer
A bad biter,
A sleepy tree climber,
A speedy food pouncer,
A man hater,
A great fighter,
A loud growler,
A fast drinker,
A sloppy eater,
A night lover,
A deer chaser,
A buffalo eater,
A child scarer,
A fluffy monster,
A wild beamer,
A fierce snarler,
A mountain climber,
A tree ruler.

Lillian Nuttall (8)
St James' CE Primary School, Clitheroe

Robin Hood

Robin Hood,
Is very, very good,
He takes from the rich and gives to the poor
And he is an outlaw.

Chloe Ross (8)
St James' CE Primary School, Clitheroe

Monkey

A brilliant shouter,
A sweet lover,
A big brained builder,
A noisy sleeper,
A playing monster,
A fast jumper,
A hairy tree eater,
A thinking stranger,
A strong muncher,
An eating terrier,
A greedy hunter,
A caring mother,
A meat hater,
A water drinker,
A bad listener,
A hair picker,
A fun pouncer,
A mad fighter,
A good bouncer,
A damp splasher,
A tree shaker.

A monkey.

Xanthe Taylor (9)
St James' CE Primary School, Clitheroe

Shirley Bassey

Shirley Bassey, Shirley Bassey,
She is so classy,
Diamonds Are Forever is my favourite song,
But every time I hear it,
I always sing it wrong.

Rachel Harnick (9)
St James' CE Primary School, Clitheroe

Lion

A big leaper,
An animal thriller,
A meat catcher,
A long pouncer,
A heavy sleeper,
A man killer,
A loud shouter,
A golden runner,
A brilliant fighter,
A good hider,
A mound climber,
A viscous biter,
A dirty digger,
A furry cuddler.

Cameron Starkie (8)
St James' CE Primary School, Clitheroe

Dogs

A tail wagger,
A fast eater,
A dragging leader,
A quiet howler,
A sneaky pincher,
A pet lover,
A kennel biter,
A loud growler,
A bone eater,
A cat hunter,
A loud cryer.

James Scorah (7)
St James' CE Primary School, Clitheroe

Rabbits

A cute cuddler,
A fast hopper,
A speedy muncher
A fast cruncher,
A furry hopper,
A veg eater,
A carrot lover,
A fast racer,
An early waker,
A heavy sleeper,
A lion hater,
A nasty scratcher.

Chloe Warburton (7)
St James' CE Primary School, Clitheroe

Dog

A fast runner,
A cat hunter,
A mad eater,
A fat walker,
A bad snorer,
A good howler,
A loud growler,
A loud muncher,
A good sniffer,
A four-legged walker.

Olivia Houghton (8)
St James' CE Primary School, Clitheroe

Snake

A quick hunter,
A smooth slither,
A poisonous killer,
A desert lover,
A slow mover,
A smart hunter,
A tree hanger,
A mouse eater,
A bug eater.

Jenna-Alexandra Sefton-Bell (8)
St James' CE Primary School, Clitheroe

Trees

Trees stand in the wind and whisper to each other,
Arms of wood ready to hug you,
Standing there looking around,
Staring at everything,
Trees look silent but in the night,
They come alive and dance around,
And when they're happy, they will wave at you,
Guarding the wood like little soldiers,
Happy living with each other.

Abigail Prescott (10)
St Joseph's Catholic Primary School, Wigan

Snakes

S nakes are smooth and scaly,
N ot slimy!
A re you afraid of snakes?
K eeping their secret lives,
E erie listening and flickering tongue . . .
S nakes are the best.

Libby Bennett (9)
St Joseph's Catholic Primary School, Wigan

The Day I Met An Alien

The day I met an alien,
He landed in a field,
He had four googly eyes,
And he carried a silver shield.

His nose was green and slimy,
His hair was blue and frizzy,
His spaceship was at the side of him,
The flashing lights made me dizzy!

I offered him a biscuit,
As I wanted him as my friend,
He said his name was Mup-Mup,
And he'd drive me round the bend.

We set off in his spaceship,
He dropped me off at school,
I was so embarrassed,
But my friends thought he was cool!

He came into my classroom,
And found himself a seat,
My mates could not believe it,
'Just look at the size of his feet!'

But he got a little home sick,
And then began to cry,
He climbed aboard his spaceship,
And flew off into the sky.

Meghan Pollitt (10)
St Joseph's Catholic Primary School, Wigan

Joy!

Joy is a handful of money,
As sweet as a cherry could be,
Joy reminds me of a bright sunny yellow,
And jumping with giggles and glee!

Joy feels like a big fluffy hug,
Given to you from your mum,
Joy is like you playing with your friends
And dancing around in the sun!

Joy smells the scent of your favourite sweet
That you eat when your homework is done,
Joy is when you hear the buzz of bees
While you're eating your lunch, having fun!

Ruby Duncan (10)
St Mary's CE (A) School, Saddleworth

My Pen

Sometimes chewed,
Doodling when bored,
Scribbles, loops, twirls,
Speeds across pages and slowly scrawls.

Stabs the page as it does full stops,
Very useful for dot to dots,
Writes its best for birthday cards,
And doing kisses and love hearts,
It writes letters and special forms,
And diary at bed, before it yawns.

Fionn Wall (10)
St Mary's CE (A) School, Saddleworth

Happiness

It's pink like pansies, swaying in the sun,
It sounds like children having fun,
It tastes like sugar, really sweet,
It sounds like dancing, feel the beat,
It feels like silk, smooth to the touch,
As cute as a little rabbit away in his hutch.

It reminds me of Laura, she is my friend,
And when she starts laughing she never ends!

Kate Gardner (10)
St Mary's CE (A) School, Saddleworth

The Witches' Spell

(Based on Macbeth)

*'Double, double, toil and trouble,
Fire burn and cauldron bubble'.*

Fillet of a smelly snack,
In the cauldron, boil and boil,
Eye of a person and tongue of a dog,
A smelly bone and wasp sting,
And a soup with trouble,
School in a desert in a bubble,
School in the desert in trouble.

*Double, double, toil and trouble,
Fire burn and cauldron bubble.*

Rebecca Baxendale (7)
Whittle-Le-Woods CE Primary School, Chorley

The Witches' Spell
(Based on Macbeth)

*'Double, double, toil and trouble,
Fire burn and cauldron bubble'.*

Horrible bugs,
Gruesome slugs,
Pencil leads
And vampire heads.

Croaky frogs,
Boggy bogs,
Scampering rats,
And hairy bats.

*'Double, double, toil and trouble,
Fire burn and cauldron bubble.'*

Emma Dixon (7)
Whittle-Le-Woods CE Primary School, Chorley

The Witches' Spell
(Based on 'Macbeth')

*'Double, double, toil and trouble,
Fire burn and cauldron bubble'.*

Mix in a dog's tongue and it will never go wrong,
100 tarantulas with hairy legs,
Head of a dog, and a frog's leg,
4 rat tails and slimy dogs' legs,
With rat tongues with boys' heads.

*'Double, double, toil and trouble,
Fire burn and cauldron bubble.'*

Morgan Cooper (7)
Whittle-Le-Woods CE Primary School, Chorley

Double, Double, Toil And Trouble

Flies eyes and meat pies,
Eggs and dogs' legs,
What will come next?
Rats' tails, smelly snails,
Bats' wings, bee stings,
Slimy ducks and witches' boots.

Jordan Rushton (8)
Whittle-Le-Woods CE Primary School, Chorley

The Dolphin

The dolphin, the dolphin,
He is very cool!

He has a slippery blue body too,
And he dips in the pool,
But his smooth body is too cute,
And he does a groovy dance,
And he plays the flute.

Anna Billingsley (7)
Whittle-Le-Woods CE Primary School, Chorley

The Monkey

The monkey, the monkey,
He collects bees,
He has fleas and his armpits smell of peas,
And he flies through the trees,
But his hair is green,
And he smells of cheese,
And he has all sorts of keys.

Oliver Darby (8)
Whittle-Le-Woods CE Primary School, Chorley

The Dog

The dog, the dog,
She's very funny, when I get home she comes to me,
She has green eyes,
And she eats my pies,
But her fur is white
And she really bites,
And she's a very nice friend and that's the
End!

Olivia Wilkes (8)
Whittle-Le-Woods CE Primary School, Chorley

The Bionic Bunny

The bionic bunny - the bionic bunny,
He is really cute,
He has a bushy tail
And he is half-mute,
But his tail is fluffy
And his teeth are so white
And he is far from a whale in size.

Sam Barber (7)
Whittle-Le-Woods CE Primary School, Chorley

The Witches Spell
(Based on Macbeth)

'Double, double, toil and trouble,
Fire burn and cauldron bubble'.

A leg of a rat and a wing of a bat,
We stir the cauldron with a curl of a girl,
The head of a frog and a head of a dog,
As we watched the worm squirm in the pot.

Deagan Greenacre (7)
Whittle-Le-Woods CE Primary School, Chorley

The Horse, The Horse!

The horse, the horse,
He trots through the woods,
He has a lovely mane,
And he likes hay,
But his birthday is in May,
And sometimes he's naughty,
But he's still the best!

Rebecca Bamber (8)
Whittle-Le-Woods CE Primary School, Chorley

The Monkey

The monkey, the monkey,
He swings in the trees,
He has a long tail
And lives in the breeze,
But his long arms are strong,
And carry him far,
And sleeps under the stars.

Ben Hall (8)
Whittle-Le-Woods CE Primary School, Chorley

The Witches' Spell

A head of a bat and a leg of a rat,
A bit of a fly
And a spider's web,
The eye of a fly and a human bone,
Is something missing?
A frog's jump added to the brew,
A worm who squirms.

John Bennett (7)
Whittle-Le-Woods CE Primary School, Chorley

Wizard's Recipe

Slimy slugs and green slime,
Goblin snot to make your soup,
But to make the perfect recipe,
You always have to have a monster's stinky socks
And his very dirty knickers,
Now last but not least,
The final ingredients - you!

Harvey Fisher (8)
Whittle-Le-Woods CE Primary School, Chorley

The Horse, The Horse

The horse, the horse,
He has long, wavy hair,
He had a lovely bear,
And he had four hooves,
But his treats are in the shape of hooves,
And he has a woolly scarf,
And he likes to play with calves.

Jessica Buff (7)
Whittle-Le-Woods CE Primary School, Chorley

Hopping Bunny

The bunny, the bunny,
Hops along,
He has long ears,
And strong feet
But his eyes are gold,
And he likes carrots,
And his fur is grey as grey can be.

Alex Fairhurst (7)
Whittle-Le-Woods CE Primary School, Chorley

The Witches' Spell

A beautiful petal of a flower,
A whole fish,
A smelly dirty head of a pig,
I'd rather have a tasty dog,
And a coat of horrible sheep,
And I'd rather a tasty pie for my tea,
And now a small hair of a frog,
And now for my last ingredient - you!

Sadie Gowan (7)
Whittle-Le-Woods CE Primary School, Chorley

The Giraffe

The giraffe, the giraffe,
He is brown and has got white spots,
He has a very cute face,
And sweet and good and beautiful,
But his coat is hot,
And I love him lots,
And he has got brown eyes.

Katie Barlow (7)
Whittle-Le-Woods CE Primary School, Chorley

Pride

Pride is blue,
Pride smells like sweet roses blooming,
Pride tastes like chocolate, sweet and satisfying,
Pride sounds like birds chirping,
Pride feels soft and smooth,
Pride lives in our hearts.

Sophie Ruth Fowler (10)
Withnell Fold Primary School, Chorley

Paul, My Long-Lost Brother

Yesterday I went to church with my dark red poppy,
The vicar told tales of young men in dreadful wars,
Then a vision came to mind of Paul, my long-lost brother,
He left to fight and said goodbye, goodbye forever,
One year later, his mates came home,
But Paul never did,
Freddy, Paul's mate told of all the shooting,
Of all the bodies, of all the blood, of all the sadness,
Of how he wept,
Yesterday I went to church with my dark red poppy,
The vicar told tales of young men in dreadful wars,
Then a vision came to mind of once when I cried,
Paul is gone was what I thought,
That was all I knew.

Gabriela Sharp (10)
Withnell Fold Primary School, Chorley

Cheese

Cheese is so wiffy but still so nice,
And is also loved by little mice,
They love it for the texture and smell,
And I love it, oh so well,
Cheese is so nice,
So very nice,
And it also comes in hot and spice.

Cheese is so nice, so very nice,
It can come in all shapes and sizes,
Cheddar like a semi-circle,
Wensleydale like a square,
In each cheese there is a sensation,
Chewy, smooth, rich or creamy.

Lewis Hawkes (10)
Withnell Fold Primary School, Chorley

Perseverance

Everyone needs to persevere,
And I need to persevere to get better at things,
Whether it's guitar, sport or temper keeping,
Everyone needs to persevere.

Everyone needs to persevere,
As we'll find new things to do,
It may be a sport, tennis or rugby,
It may be getting through hard times in life,
But really it doesn't matter,
Everyone just needs to persevere,
And they will be able to do anything.

Zoë Mather (9)
Withnell Fold Primary School, Chorley

Remembrance Poem

When I went to town yesterday,
I saw a stall of poppies,
Then I remembered the war,
I was in the murky trench,
Full of water and mist,
I turned my head,
And bang, my friend was dead,
I carried him off the battlefield,
Looking at his injured leg,
I was in shock,
But I had to leave him dead,
Noises went through my head,
I didn't know what to do,
So I just ran out of the trench,
Onto the battlefield,
I saw another friend fall down,
But luckily he survived!

Lucy Davis (11)
Withnell Fold Primary School, Chorley

Apples, Apples, Apples

Apples, apples,
Juicy apples,
How they taste so sweet,
If you bite into one,
It tastes so great!
So eat one every day.

Apples, apples,
Juicy apples,
They are such a treat,
If you try eating one,
It tastes really yum!
And they are so healthy too.

Apples, apples,
Juicy apples,
They are perfect and round,
If you feel one,
They are so smooth!
So eat one every day.

Isobel Ryde (10)
Withnell Fold Primary School, Chorley

Happiness

Happiness is gold,
It smells like summer flowers,
It tastes like sweet honey,
Happiness sounds like cheering football fans,
It feels soft and gentle,
Happiness is in the heart of the sun.

James Guy (10)
Withnell Fold Primary School, Chorley

Silver

The silver moon,
Shining on a silver spoon,
Seeping through the window,
Onto the handle of the clock,
Passing onto the toy cock.

Silver lake,
Silver sweets on a cake,
Glittering like a jewel,
The wind is getting pretty cool.

The world is in bed,
Resting their head,
Silver cover,
Silver pillows,
The silver moon,
Shining on a silver spoon.

Joanna Nicholas (10)
Withnell Fold Primary School, Chorley

I Hate Dying

When people die, it makes us cry,
When people die, we start to lie,
I think to myself just about life,
As I think who needs a bad life,
As much as I hate the word knife,
It makes me twitch,
It makes me itch,
And it makes everyone sad.

I hate dying, oh yes I do,
I hate dying, just as much as you.

Davie Beesley (10)
Withnell Fold Primary School, Chorley

The Day My Life Changed

I was at church yesterday,
I remembered the day my friend was praying,
He was praying that he would be there the next day,
But in the night, my friend and I,
Went to fight for our lives,
I succeeded but my friend sadly died,
I tried, oh how I tried to save him,
I had no success,
I pulled him back to the trench,
And I broke down, I wanted my friend back,
That day the war ended,
I was the one that had to tell his family,
My life changed and never was the same again.

Emily Chaplin (10)
Withnell Fold Primary School, Chorley

Remembrance

I was shopping one day,
Everywhere I went I saw red,
Suddenly I was with my friend in the war,
We were in the Air Force,
I was in a plane next to my friend,
Then we saw an aircraft coming for us,
I was scared,
We were hit,
I was falling,
I thought it was the end,
But it wasn't for me,
It was my friend who lost his life.

Amy Wood (9)
Withnell Fold Primary School, Chorley

Remembrance Poem

I was walking to church on a Sunday morning,
When I saw a man selling poppies,
Then I remembered when I was there,
I did not have any choice,
I had to go,
I hated it,
I was walking with my gun in my trembling hand,
Hearing bombs constantly and seeing flashing lights,
Mud, rain and the murky trenches and seeing my
friends drop to the ground,
I did not have anyone else,
I was scared,
I wanted to go home and see my family again.

Lois Waterhouse (9)
Withnell Fold Primary School, Chorley

Change

I want to change wars,
Pollution too,
And so should you, change them too,
Speeding, alcohol, they can kill,
Let's stop bullying, we will stop it together,
And grumpy people who are down in the dumps,
Let's get rid of arguments and fights.

Without these changes, we cannot relax,
Come on let's change the world.

Charlie Adams (10)
Withnell Fold Primary School, Chorley

Difficulties

Difficult was when my friend moved away,
And when my dog was too old to play,
I didn't have anything to do,
Apart from play with the laces on my shoe.

Difficult was when I got my first SATs sheet,
I was very nervous and jigged around in my seat,
But when my sister changed, she didn't talk to me at all!
And when we went to the park, she didn't play football!

But at the moment, everything is great!
And my sister's attitude, well she's my mate!

Fergus Tallon (11)
Withnell Fold Primary School, Chorley

The Silver Moon

The silver moon floats in the sky,
A shining diamond it is like,
The fish swimming as bright as light,
Silver stream running down,
A jewelled pathway in the drive,
The trees glimpsing in the night,
It is a beauty,
It hurts your eyes,
What a shining view.

Josh Eckersley (11)
Withnell Fold Primary School, Chorley

Changes

It was hard going to New Zealand,
I had to leave all my friends behind,
I thought I wouldn't be able to find,
The strength inside, so I wouldn't cry,
I lived there for quite a long time,
I made new friends but they weren't the same.

It was hard going to New Zealand,
I had to leave all my friends behind,
And I really like my primary school,
Back in England, it's really cool,
It was hard to find the strength inside,
To leave my old life behind.

But now I'm back in England,
And all set for high school,
It's going to be fantastic,
And I really hope I do well.

Kai Fox (10)
Withnell Fold Primary School, Chorley

Young Writers Information

We hope you have enjoyed reading this book - and that you will continue to enjoy it in the coming years.

If you like reading and writing poetry drop us a line, or give us a call, and we'll send you a free information pack.

Alternatively if you would like to order further copies of this book or any of our other titles, then please give us a call or log onto our website at
www.youngwriters.co.uk

**Young Writers Information
Remus House
Coltsfoot Drive
Peterborough
PE2 9JX**

(01733) 890066